EST. 1967

Bailey

FLOWER ESSENCES

HANDBOOK

OF BAILEY FLOWER ESSENCES

BY

ARTHUR BAILEY

First Published in UK in 1996
Copyright © Arthur Bailey 1996 - 2004
ISBN 0 9536021 3 3

Edition 1   1996
Edition 2   1999
Edition 3   2000
Edition 4   2004

PUBLISHED BY
BAILEY FLOWER ESSENCES LTD
7 Nelson Road, Ilkley, West Yorkshire LS29 8HN

Designed by Emma Garry.
Printed and bound by Lamberts Print & Design, Station Road, Settle, North Yorkshire BD24 9AA

contents

preface to the fourth edition

In spite of my best efforts to stop the number of essences from growing, there have been some new additions since the last edition of the handbook four years ago. What is noticeable is that these new essences are mainly for raising levels of consciousness or freeing us from negative influences locked within the cells of the body.

Personal progress seems to be controlled by two factors: old controlling patterns from the past and new energies for change appearing in the present. The need for change at a personal level seems to be growing rapidly. Old methods of working are becoming rapidly outmoded. In the fields of politics and political leadership the need for major change has never been seen more clearly.

Inertia from past conditionings and a lack of intuitive energising are the factors that hold people back from progressing in their lives. The new essences that have been developed in the last four years are particularly helpful in these areas.

We are often held back from making progress by patterns which seem to be locked within the very cells of the body. Often these are controlled by deep-rooted subconscious fears and terrors which can inhibit our progress to a new and brighter future. Several of the new essences are particularly helpful in freeing us from the tyranny of these old imprinted patterns.

We also need to be able to find new ways of maintaining progress. It is all too easy to fall back into old habitual patterns because of their familiarity, because we feel secure with them. These then subvert our ability to make positive changes to our lives.

In the East there is a traditional time of change and cleansing called the Kali Yuga, which occurs every 2,000 years, often with great upheaval and distress. We are now in a Kali Yuga period and the increased instability and upheaval is all too obvious. Catharsis is never pleasant - we all like peace and stability. Yet, as the Buddha noted, everything changes ceaselessly (whether we like it or not!).

I hope that the set of the Bailey essences now addresses the needs of people at this difficult time. The essences encourage positive ways of change, of moving forward leaving outmoded ways behind and embracing new and brighter ways of living our lives.

As I have discovered in my own life, the hidden powers within the flowers and plants around us are totally amazing. There is a wisdom and healing power that goes way beyond the traditional teaching of botanists and herbalists.

The beauty of flower essences is that they never push, they never compel us. Rather, it is as if they suggest things to us. They are more like wise guides who point out the way, guides that we can ignore if we so wish. Flower essences are therefore totally dissimilar to drugs which impose their effects on the mind-body system. They are equally different from pharmaceutical drugs in that they act on the whole body-mind-spirit complex - as well as on the links with one's true soul.

Dr Edward Bach, the founder of the modern flower essence revolution, was ahead of his time and unfortunately never saw the real fruits of his labours. Nowadays, flower essences are many and diverse. They are difficult to categorise because of their much wider fields of application. Modern essences go far beyond just treating emotional states; indeed many of them are concerned with man's spiritual quest in this strange and bewildering universe.

Conventional medicine now seems to be concerned largely with drug therapy and the spiritual aspects of health are ignored, except as side effects. Yet if we are spiritually unfulfilled then there will inevitably be a sense of futility in our lives and our health will suffer accordingly. It is in this area that flower essences can be so helpful. We must make sure, if at all possible, that these aids to spiritual growth are not trampled underfoot by being legislated out of existence - this is a very real threat within the EU. Unfortunately, the EU is not controlled by the EU parliament but by non-elected commissioners who formulate, and have the last say on legislation. These commissioners are also immune from prosecution - an infallible recipe for underhand dealings and corruption. The structure is very like that of the old Soviet Union! If the worst does happen and flower essences largely become banned (the cost of licensing would be prohibitive for most producers) then we will have to move our sales offshore and only trade as a mail-order company. One thing is sure: we will not readily be shut down by authoritarian diktats from Brussels or anywhere else.

However, at the present time we are still able to function as before and over the last four years have developed powerful new essences. These are:- Sacred Lotus, Bladder Senna, Round Headed Leek, Cyprus Rock Rose, Meadow Rue, Dwarf Purple Vetch and Conifer Mazegill. All of these fill needs that were not fully covered by the existing range.

We are also now marketing a Stressbuster and Space Harmoniser that neutralises negative energies such as Geopathic Stress. Negative earth energies can seriously undermine health and so far I know of no flower essences that can remove these negative effects. This electronic device has taken five years to perfect and gives very good results. Full details are given on our website.

Flowers still have new messages for me, new insights. They are complex beautiful beings, and they do not reveal all their secrets at once. Perhaps that is one of the most wonderful aspects of flower essence healing - knowing that changes will go on. There is no final end to such insights. I am told that Dr Bach knew that, and is reputed to have told Victor Bullen that at least one of his own series was most likely only temporary. He felt that something more powerful would later come to replace it.

Some of the descriptions have been modified since the last edition of the handbook. This is not because the previous descriptions were incorrect, but because other factors needed to be involved. In particular the positive aspects of the essences are now stressed more fully. The negative aspects of essences can be helpful in arriving at a symptom diagnosis, yet the positive aspects are much more encouraging to the client. "Widening one's horizons" is much more attractive than "being narrow minded"! Being called a "miserable sinner" does not really stimulate us to make positive change in our lives, it is far more likely to make us feel inadequate or guilty, and so block our progress.

We greatly appreciate all the feedback that we get from people who use the essences. It helps to stimulate our search for new ways of helping people. In particular we appreciate the very clear comments that some people have made regarding the descriptions of the essences. Thank you very much for all your continuing support and encouragement.

We now have a website that we hope honours the beauty and power of the flowers and plants that we use.

The site - www.baileyessences.com - took much time and effort to create, but we feel that it was a very worthwhile task. Those of you with internet access will find all the flowers listed, complete with photographs and full descriptions of them.

ARTHUR BAILEY
June 2004

8

a personal note

As a child I was always drawn towards flowers. I was fascinated by all their different colours, smells and shapes. To me they were beautiful and somehow mysterious. This love of nature was further stimulated by George Ringer, the husband of my grandmother's housekeeper. We used to go for long walks in the woods and on the fells near Grange-over-Sands and there were very few flowers or trees that he did not know by name. It was in many ways a magical time.

Then things changed. There was no place in the school curriculum for the study of nature. It was all the three 'R's, languages, science, etc. Gradually these things began to dominate my life. I took an interest in science and found it easy. It was a subject in which I could excel and also something my parents knew little about, so that decided my future. Looking back I can now see that my parents tried too hard to bring my brother and me up as model human beings. Inevitably that sowed the seeds of a quiet rebellion within me.

I became an engineering scientist and chartered engineer. Eventually I became a Senior Lecturer in Electrical and Electronic Engineering at Bradford University. My interest in dowsing and flower essences, which developed during this period, started by accident.

Early in 1966 I contracted Asian 'flu. It was a very bad epidemic and the 'flu was particularly virulent. I was left with severe toxic symptoms that my doctor called post-viral syndrome. Having nothing better to do, I read extensively. It was in one of the books that I read that I first came across water divining. This was in a largely autobiographical book by Beverly Nicholls. Having plenty of spare time on my hands, I tried it out - not expecting anything to happen.

Much to my surprise I discovered that it actually worked. This was finally proved without question when I discovered where the water supply came in from the road and where the tarred-over stop tap was located. I then carried out a whole series of experiments, many of which were with the archaeology section at the university.

My dowsing worked time after time, both accurately and repeatedly. However, my scientific mind became very worried when I discovered that it still worked when reason said it should not. I even did a double-blind test on map-dowsing with complete accuracy. Very reluctantly I began to accept that there were things that existed that I had not dreamed possible. There was the uncomfortable fact that dowsing seemed to contravene the 'laws' of science. I finally concluded that there had to be at least two more dimensions in the universe (so far unknown to science) for dowsing to be explicable. This arises from the fact that with dowsing one is not necessarily restricted by time or distance.

It was a homeopathic doctor, the late Dr Aubrey Westlake, who finally helped me to recover from my post-viral symptoms (ME). I later read that his wife used dowsing to help him in the selection of homeopathic and flower remedies. This started me off exploring the world of flower essence healing.

In 1966 I bought a set of Bach remedies from Nora Weeks at Mount Vernon. Like Mrs Westlake, I used dowsing to determine which remedies to take. I was surprised just how accurate, in terms of emotional symptoms, the dowsing was.

It was around that time that I first met the late Major Bruce McManaway, who introduced me to laying-on-of-hands healing. I discovered that I could feel through my hands where people had physical problems. Not only that, but their health usually improved when I kept my hands on the places where I felt the reactions. This I found even more unnerving than dowsing!

Gradually an increasing number of people came to me for help and I used both the Bach remedies and hand healing. However, there were times when none of the Bach remedies seemed suitable for a particular client. Yet something inside me insisted that there were flowers that could help them. So early in 1967 I began to investigate other flowers for their curative properties. I started by dowsing over the plants in our large garden. Five of them gave very positive results. I made essences from these by using Dr Bach's "sun" method.

I started dowsing over my own essences as well as the Bach ones and used them when they came up in my dowsing. Rather to my surprise they helped my clients a great deal, even though at that time I did not know what they were for! All my attempts to discover their properties met with a blank. Certainly they were not for emotional states like the Bach ones. However, the remedies obviously worked and the range steadily expanded, often in response to the needs of a client when no other essences were indicated.

I also discovered that some plants, like the Firethorn, gave good results when the fruits were used. For this type of plant material I found alcohol extraction to be the most effective method. Indeed, it produced more powerful essences from some flowers as well.

Initially I kept my discoveries to myself. This was due to self-doubt rather than secretiveness. However, once they had proved to be effective I began to give the information to others and started to sell the essences.

At this point I spent a considerable time agonising about what to call them. 'The Yorkshire Essences' was one possibility - yet the flowers had come from many places, from Scotland to Cornwall. I therefore decided that, as I was taking responsibility for them and describing their properties, I should give them my name.

I finally discovered the main properties of these first "Bailey" essences through meditational insight. I realised that they were for attitudes of mind - how people see and relate to the world around them. They were therefore quite different from the Bach remedies. Indeed, it is our attitudes of mind that give rise to negative emotional states.

As the series expanded I realised that there was far more to flower essences that I had imagined. Gradually I came to realise through my own experience that we are all multi-dimensional beings. Therefore when we experience difficulties in life, the root of our problems may not be in just the body-mind area. We need to take a much broader view.

The Bailey essences are primarily concerned with personal growth and liberation. This does not mean that the essences cannot help physical illnesses - far from it. Yet their main emphasis is on helping us to integrate mind, body and spirit. We need to break the hold of the old conditionings and beliefs that can deny us our freedom. As these old patterns ease away, we need support and insight so that we can find our own true paths in life.

Many of us are severely restricted in our freedom to live life as we would wish. These restrictions usually stem from childhood, when the development of true self-confidence may be hindered. As a result we also lack understanding of our innate spiritual nature.

These flower essences help us to open our eyes and see things as they really are, to let go of fears and to discover the real power and magic that lies at the heart of each one of us - to discover more about ourselves than perhaps we ever dreamt possible. As I have discovered for myself, experience is far superior to belief.

Beliefs are usually based on what other people have told us, and may be completely untrue. Personal experience, even though it can be misinterpreted, is a far surer path. It is hard to deny what we have experienced personally.

If we are to find true happiness in this life, we need to discover our own true nature. It is here that flower essences can really help us, suggesting how we need to change. They are not drugs so they do not force change, but they will help us to change if and when we are ready for change to take place. They are therefore gentle but persuasive in their action.

general background to the essences

Most of our illnesses relate to our way of living and our attitudes to life and the world around us. Diet and environment do have a major influence on health but so also do our mental attitudes. Indeed, for many people, mental attitudes are the key factors which affect their health, for good or ill. Fears and tensions can lock up muscles, distort the skeleton, depress the immune system, affect all the endocrine secretions, and therefore compromise our health. On the other hand, if we are relaxed and coping easily with the stresses of life, then our health will benefit accordingly. Mind and body are not separate and the reactions of each depend on what is happening to the other. Indeed, they should really be called body-mind - a composite whole. Exercising the body can therefore help to clear the mind (as has been known for centuries by Yoga practitioners). Similarly, exercising the mind (as in meditation, for example) can help to free the body. Anything that can help to free up the body-mind system can thus be considered as a healing agent.

In addition, although some people deny its existence, we have a spiritual dimension. Our intuition stems from this area, and if there is disharmony here, it will spill over into our everyday lives. In this spiritual dimension we are still, however, in the realm of duality. Put simply, there are demons as well as angels! However, as in ordinary life, it is usually the apparently negative things that test us. Without such testing we never know whether our personal strengths are real or imaginary. Spiritual is not therefore superior to ordinary mundane life, but simply a part of it. There is a dimension beyond the spiritual that is non-dualistic. In different cultures this has different names - God, Allah, Buddha, Nature, The Great Spirit, etc., etc. Here, too, flowers can help us make contact with the original source of our being.

The Bailey essences help to bring about much-needed change in our life. They act as catalysts for this change, and are concerned with bringing us up to date rather than dwelling on past difficulties. They can then help us to move forward along our own true path, to sing our own particular song-life, a song of rejoicing.

They have been referred to as "new generation of flower essences", and that is indeed what they are. In truth, they bear no relation whatever to conventional allopathic medicine; their action is far wider. They are concerned with personal healing and growth at all the levels of body, mind and spirit.

There is a vital need world-wide for a radically different way of living. We are at a crossroads. We are faced with the stark choice between personal growth or disintegration of the social fabric of the world. Events throughout the world point to the fact that greed and confrontation can no longer be sustained. The powers that man has developed make this path far too dangerous. It is like playing with matches in a gunpowder store. It is very tempting to blame the politicians for our problems. But politicians will change only in response to changes in humankind. The need for such change is urgent.

In the past, approaches to personal development have often been very negative, concentrating on personal shortcomings. These methods can result in over-dependence on the system that is being used which in turn produces personal disempowerment and a consequent blocking of personal progress. This type of system is dominantly "Yang" and is concerned with authoritarian power. Now is the time for the "Yin" energies to come to the fore, with their much more compassionate ways of looking at things. People are intrinsically good, although it may not always be apparent! It is this inner worth that needs to be encouraged and flower essences can help in this process.

However, it is important to remember that we must never try to impose on others what we think they need. That can too easily become interference or invasion. People will only change when they are ready to change. As Khalil Gibran puts it in The Prophet - "No man can reveal to you aught but that which already lies half asleep in the dawning of your knowledge". The true healer is a catalyst for change, and that is what these essences are about: they are Catalysts for Change. It is as if they remind people what they have always known at a deep level but have lost touch with. They help those positive energies to reawaken ("remembering" is how the Sufis put it) and so liberate people from old negative patterns of thought and behaviour.

The original six essences have steadily expanded and changed since they were first developed in 1967. There are now 58 in the standard set at the time of writing (July 2004). Fourteen of these are composite essences which utilise several different species of flowers selected for their complementary qualities. In total, there are 95 single essences, all of which are available separately. We find that many homeopaths prefer to have the single essences rather than use the composite essences that contain them.

Feedback about any of the flower essences is always very welcome. Such information is invaluable, and helps to stimulate deeper insights into their action. Flowers, like human beings, are very complex and they have many more properties than we may realise.

The Bailey essences are perfectly compatible with, and often complementary to, many other flower essences and have given very good results over the years when used in conjunction with others. However, their main action is in "helping people to help themselves" rather than just alleviating symptoms or emotional states.

selection of the appropriate essences

NONE OF THESE ESSENCES IS INTENDED TO TREAT CLINICAL SYMPTOMS THAT ARE IN THE PROVINCE OF CONVENTIONAL WESTERN MEDICINE. IF IN DOUBT, YOU SHOULD ALWAYS CONSULT YOUR MEDICAL PHYSICIAN.

The essences relate to attitudes of mind and beliefs, rather than clinical symptoms. For this reason, there may at times be some difficulty in determining which of the essences to use. There is no particular essence that can be prescribed, for example, for a headache or for a kidney disorder. The physical symptoms displayed can vary enormously, depending on the total mind-body-spirit make-up of the client. For example, problems that occurred in childhood could result in symptoms of headache in one person and ME in another. We therefore need to go beyond symptom diagnosis in deciding which essences are the most appropriate.

The composite essences have names that give a fairly clear idea of their field of application. The single essences are all referred to by their common names, and here the name may bear little resemblance to its uses. To determine which essence or group of essences a person needs may therefore present some difficulties.

One way of choosing the most appropriate essence or essences is by counselling. The information needed from clients is about how they see the world and relate to it. For instance: Are they dominated by the authority of others? Do they have little confidence in their own judgements? If so, the Self-esteem Composite might be the most appropriate one to choose. Have they many problems that stem from childhood - indeed, are they still locked in some childhood patterns? In this case the Childhood composite could be considered. At times however, it is quite hard to ascertain exactly what is needed. Some clients keep their difficulties to themselves, or indeed may be completely unaware of the nature of their problem. Alternative prescribing methods can overcome these difficulties by removing the need to question the client. Three of these methods are listed overleaf.

[1] Muscle-Testing. This goes under several different names including Applied Kinesiology. In this method the client holds a bottle of each of the essences in turn. For each essence the strength of a group of the client's muscles is tested. This can be done by seeing whether a given force will deflect an arm or separate finger and thumb. The appropriate essences are indicated by the client's reduced resistance to the applied pressure.

[2] Dowsing. Here the practitioner needs to have an open mind, to avoid influencing the results. This detachment is vital, as auto-suggestion can seriously compromise dowsing accuracy. Most people use a pendulum for selecting the most appropriate essence. The author's book on dowsing (Anyone Can Dowse for Better Health, ISBN. 0-572-02461-4) gives full details of this method of working. "Radionics" is another form of dowsing that can be used. Radionic and other similar methods use a number-code system rather than looking for "Yes" or "No" answers. Both are equally valid and in skilled hands can give accurate results.

[3] The "Vega" Machine. This measures the electrical resistance of one of the body's acupuncture points - normally on a thumb or a big toe. Samples of the essences to be tested are placed in the instrument, one at a time. When a match is obtained, the electrical skin resistance of the acupuncture point falls appreciably. This is indicated on a meter, with an associated change of audible tone.

Whatever method is used, the final list of essences should give a thumbnail sketch of the personality of the client and the areas of difficulty in their life. From this information we can see both positive and negative aspects of the personality. The negative aspects relate to symptoms that the client may be suffering from and can be helpful for deciding which essences may be the most appropriate. I feel, however, that it is important to focus on the positive aspects when discussing matters with the client. All of us respond better to a "carrot" than a "big stick". We need to encourage our clients to look for positive change, helping them to work for a new and brighter future. The

Bailey essences encourage people to live in the present moment where they can blossom and reach their full potential in life.

Preparation of the Client's Prescription

To 10 ml of spring water (or 50% vodka 50% spring water for longer keeping properties) add 2-3 drops of each essence selected. In the case of alcohol intolerance, a solution of salt can be used instead. In this case add approximately 25% by weight of sea-salt to the spring water and shake it until all the salt has dissolved. The alcohol or salt are only present as preservatives.

The prescription is best prepared in, and then dispensed from, a dropper bottle. The client should take three drops three times per day - preferably before meals. If the middle dose is inconvenient, then twice a day is acceptable although it may take longer to see any results.

The drops can be taken directly on the tongue or in a little water. If the problems are acute, then the prescription can be taken more frequently - every hour or so if needed. This is most likely where sudden shock has occurred, for example where there has been an accident or a bereavement.

A 10 ml bottle will last approximately three weeks when used as directed. Normally it is best for the whole bottle to be taken. However, if symptoms are changing rapidly it may be advisable to check more frequently - say, every week - and adjust the prescription to reflect the client's changing energies.

The essences are also effective if the drops are rubbed into the soft skin areas of the body such as the inner wrists or behind the ears.

The essences are entirely suitable for children; no change in dose is needed.

Animals also respond very well to the flower essences. Drops can be put direct on food or in drinking water. Alternatively, they can be put on skin on the ears for example. Small animals can take the same dose as humans; animals as large as horses do rather better when the number of drops is multiplied by three.

If no dropper bottles are available, then two drops of each of the selected essences can be added to a small glass of water. A small amount of this can then be sipped three times per day. If it is kept refrigerated, this mixture has a useful life of about three days, after which a new mixture will need to be prepared.

Alternatively, two drops of each of the stock essences being used can be taken directly by mouth. With the Shock & Trauma composite, this is the preferred way of taking the essence. The stock concentrations are such that they do not need to be diluted before use. Because of the "homeopathic" concentrations of the essences, the activity of a fully diluted medicine prepared from the stock essences is similar to that of the stock essences themselves.

Up to five essences can be given at any one time. More than this is not normally recommended, but I have given up to ten different essences at a time when they were indicated. Rules for flower essences are only rough working guides. Here it should be noted that the composite essences can be treated in exactly the same way as a single essence. If more than five appear to be needed, then it may be better to split the essences into two separate prescriptions. These could then be taken in alternate weeks, or the two prescriptions could be alternated day by day.

Having established this as a general guideline, I think it is important to note that this is not always the case and sometimes more essences are needed. The method used to select the appropriate essences should be trusted.

The Bailey Flower Essences
methodology

Although the initial inspiration for the Bailey essences was the work of Dr Bach, they are not produced in quite the same way. The "boiling" method has been replaced with alcohol extraction, which gives a more rounded quality to the essences. This is most likely due to aromatic compounds being dissolved in the alcohol, rather than being driven off by the boiling process.

We use the "sun" method for most of the essences. We find that even in winter we get powerful essences, if we pick a bright sunny day.

At first the Bach rates of dilution were used. However, after some checks by dowsing, it was discovered that greater potency could be obtained by a different procedure. Instead of diluting straight from the original "mother tincture" to the stock bottles, a two-stage dilution was evolved. This has proved to be beneficial in giving greater potency to the finished stock essences. It appears that some potency is lost if too great a dilution is achieved in a single stage. The reason for this is not clear, but it may be related to the way that water absorbs the information from the original herbal extract.

The two-stage dilution corresponds approximately to a 2C homeopathic dilution for each stage. That is an approximate 10,000:1 dilution from mother tincture to stock bottle (two stages each of about 100:1). The first dilution from mother tincture we term our "daughter" tincture. The second stage of dilution is the finished stock bottle.

We also give a few succussions to the daughter tinctures after preparing them from the mother tincture. This is not essential, but it does give a more "solid" feel to the final stock essence.

All the essences are hand-made by our family using pure spring water and vodka as the base. We use vodka rather than brandy, as vodka is just very pure alcohol, whereas the quality of brandy varies greatly depending on its manufacturer. In addition, brandy includes a large variety of compounds from both the original distillation and the oak casks used for ageing. There is a possibility that some of these may be detrimental to the quality of the final essence.

We feel very strongly that the quality of all essences of homeopathic concentration is greatly influenced by the care taken at all stages of their preparation. In the production of the essences it is our aim to honour the inherent healing potential of the flowers to the greatest possible degree.

Although homeopathic dilution rates have been quoted above, these flower essences are not homeopathic as most people understand the word. As far as we know, in high concentrations they do not produce the "symptoms" of the state that one is trying to alleviate. In this they are similar to other flower essences in that they have to be proved (i.e. tested) by actual use.

All the essences are standardised by dowsing methods during preparation so that all batches of stock essences have the same potency.

In the following list of essences, the method used to make the essence is shown. Where there is no mention of a method, the traditional sun method has been used.

Those made by alcohol extraction are marked with an (A) after the botanical name. In this method, the plant material is collected and soaked in vodka. The plant material is then strained off, and the remaining liquid is the mother tincture.

Cymbidium Orchid is made in a similar way to the sun method but is made overnight in our meditation room by the light of the full moon. This method is marked (M).

Not all the essences are made from flowers. A few are produced from the fruit or the leaves of a plant. These are indicated by the initial (F) for fruit or (L) for leaf after the botanical name of the plant.

Important Notice

These essences are not medicines as the word is normally understood. They are not intended to cure or alleviate any medical condition. If in doubt, always consult your regular medical practitioner.

Their mode of operation is to help to rebalance the mind-body-spirit unity of the person taking them. However, physical health and symptoms are related to the internal harmony within the being, so improvements in clinical conditions may well be experienced.

They are catalysts for change, not medicines that impose their effects on the body. Because of this, their action will vary widely from person to person depending on the individual circumstances.

the essences

* Essences that are part of the standard full set

KEY:
(A) Alcohol extraction
(L) Leaf
(P) Whole plant
(F) Fruit
(M) Made by moonlight

All other essences prepared from flowers by the sun method.

ALMOND* *(Prunus dulcis)*

This is the flower of the inner teacher, the guide. Almond helps us to disentangle ourselves from past difficulties, and then to see our path ahead. It forms links with our soul, our very essence. Inevitably it will challenge us, because beliefs from the past often have a strange attraction for us - even though deep down we know they are restricting our freedom. The new path is unknown territory. As old familiar identities are left behind we will feel less and less bound by our past. In extreme cases we may not even recognise ourselves. This indeed would be the stuff of bad dreams and nightmares if we were not in safe hands. On such a journey we need the comfort, support and reassurance of a guide who will urge us ever onwards towards our own ultimate blossoming and freedom. We need to establish a true sense of our own worth, to find our true self-confidence so that we can become "self-programming", immune to the opposition of others who feel threatened by our changing personality. We need to learn how to rely on our own intuition. Particularly we need to learn how to discriminate between true intuition and the false images created by the ego.

Almond essence helps to liberate us from old patterns that have had us dancing to their tune. It is a gentle essence but very deep. Many of the spring essences have this same characteristic, that of gentleness. There is a certain maximum speed at which we can progress along our own path. Compassion and love dictate that we must not exceed that speed. What we are looking for is encouraging change in people, not imposing it on them. Almond helps us to ease away from old patterns, but it also enables us to see, in detachment, how those patterns arose. It can also help us to understand what benefits we actually gained during those restricting times in the past.

ANGER AND FRUSTRATION*

RED POPPY *(Papaver argemone)*, FIRETHORN *(Pyracantha atalantioides)* (F) (A), HOLLY LEAF *(Ilex aquifolium)* (L) (A)

We all need energy. Too much energy expressed and we become angry, too little and we become ineffective. We need our energy to be in balance. This composite helps us to achieve that in several ways.

Red Poppy enables us to build up our reserves of energy. Some people are so frightened of the potentially destructive power of anger that they live their lives at half-power, frightened to come out into the open. Red Poppy helps to bring up our energy levels in a controlled manner.

Firethorn is there to stabilise our energies so that we are able to express ourselves clearly, and if necessary forcefully, without overreaction.

Holly Leaf is for frustration. When we are frustrated our anger turns inward and we become defensively prickly. Holly Leaf helps to protect us so that we do not rise to the bait so easily, and so we avoid over-reaction.

Overall, this essence encourages us to live our lives more fully as we become more able to take control of our emotional reactions to the situations we meet.

ARIZONA FIR* *(Abies lasiocarpa var. compacta)*

In many religions it is assumed that any enjoyment of life is "not spiritual", that life should be hard. Indeed, any enjoyment of life is seen as a severe stumbling block on one's path. Such ascetic teachings are distortions of the Truth. Clinging to a path of suffering and mortification can be just as disastrous to one's personal growth as living the life of a hedonist. It is the clinging that is the problem, not what one is clinging to. What is needed is balance.

Many people do not enjoy their lives. For them, life is full of woe and suffering. Yet, viewed differently, it can be seen as an amazing and wonderful experience - something to be enjoyed. The essence of Arizona Fir is about celebrating life and existence. It can stimulate a sense of freedom and joy. It is only when we can really open up and rejoice that the Heart Chakra (which represents love) can be fully energised. We need to be able to love life and to love our own selves, warts and all, celebrating life as spiritual beings, whilst living on this earth. There is nothing wrong with enjoying ourselves; it is the attachment to such enjoyment that is the problem. When we can dance in celebration and we, the dancer, no longer exist, then there is only the dance. That is true celebration. In such timelessness there is no ego, just a unity with all creation. Arizona Fir softens our rigidity and opens the door to the mysteries of true celebration.

BETONY *(Stachys officinalis) - Component of Fears*

Betony is for unrecognisable and unidentifiable fears. These are the deep fears of the subconscious that hide from us yet, at times, can dominate our lives. These forces can make us feel unworthy, unloved or unwanted. In extreme cases, such fears can drive people to contemplate suicide. They cut us off from recognising our own true worth. They may appear as fear of demons, devils, "the devil within", the shadow side of our own being. They may also derive from childhood conditioning where we may have been led to believe that we are inherently evil – full of "original sin". Freud saw the subconscious as a repository of negative suppressed impulses. He did not realise that it is also the area of inner wisdom and light. We need to be able to shed light compassionately on those inner "demons" and then see them for what they are - just old thought-forms that have no real substance. Betony enables us to discover this inner truth so that we can go beyond the traps of such negative thinking. Once we become freed from old subconscious fears, then we are able to experience much more fully the glory of being alive. We then see that we have a golden opportunity to grow and develop in this amazing workshop we call Earth.

BISTORT* *(Polygonum bistorta) (A) – Component of Transition*
Bistort helps those who are at a major change-point in their lives, where old ways of relating to the world are under pressure from new and more relevant ones. At times of severe personal crisis people may arrive at a point where they suffer from a "nervous breakdown". They are being mentally challenged and their old ways of being are no longer working for them. Maybe they need to be able to come up-front and assert themselves. Bistort can help to convert a possible breakdown into a "breakthrough". It also helps to awaken love and self-protection at times of major emotional upheaval. For many people, these times of personal crisis are very traumatic, often giving rise to negativity and depression. "Why should this happen to me?" is the cry that is often expressed. This negativity can be self-destructive as people progressively withdraw from sources of possible help, even becoming suicidal. Bistort helps to provide an inner scaffolding that maintains the basic structure of the personality and provides loving support during the processes of change. It is important to give positive encouragement to people undergoing traumatic changes in their lives. These times are like the pain of giving birth - in this case it is the possible birth of a new and more positive way of living. This essence can be very empowering, helping people to develop the internal resolve and power needed to rise above their difficulties.

BLACK LOCUST* *(Robinia pseudoacacia L.)*
In the spring, this tree with the rather strange name has beautiful fragrant flowers from which the essence is made. This is the essence of choice when we feel vulnerable to the attacks, or undesired attentions, of other people. These can be quite varied, depending on circumstances.

It may be that we feel we are the victims of "psychic attack", that, for whatever reason, someone wants to get back at us and we are being affected at the psychic level. It can be due to jealousy or anger or some other powerful emotion. Often the people responsible are not even aware that their thoughts can affect others from a distance.

It may be that we feel smothered or angered by the attentions of someone else. Again, their emotional reactions can have exactly the same effect - that of generating feelings of being attacked, of being vulnerable. Victims of stalkers often fall into this category.

It matters not whether we, either as the recipient or the perpetrator, believe or disbelieve in the possibility of psychic attack. My experience is that it can happen even when neither person believes in the possibility! James Neil, a policeman (author of Ju-Ju in my Life), went out to work in Ghana disbelieving in the power of witch-doctors. He discovered to his cost that disbelief did not prevent him from becoming a victim.

So if ever one feels seriously depleted with no obvious cause, or when some form of psychic interference is suspected, this is the essence to use. As well as its fragrant blossoms, the tree has large protective thorns! The essence mirrors these characteristics, broadcasting healing energies to others, as well as ourselves, whilst protecting us from undesired attentions.

BLACKTHORN *(Prunus spinosa) - Component of Depression & Despair*

Blackthorn is for the ultimate state of despair. Here we feel to be in a deep dark pit with no way out. All seems lost; neither life nor death has any meaning. Sometimes we may feel that we are travelling through the "Valley of the Shadow of Death". This is the ultimate point of the "self-destruct" mechanism of the personality. It is the point where all our illusions have been shattered by the force of outside circumstances. Blackthorn mirrors this feeling with its sharp black thorns. Yet from these depths a completely new growth into a much lighter way of living is possible, leaving the old destructive ways behind. There is a dawn beyond the darkest night; it is only our fears that prevent us from seeing the light. The black pit may well have been generated by a strong ego finding itself in conflict with the force of outside circumstances. It is the conflict between strongly held personal opinions and Truth (as it is experienced in our lives) that can finally precipitate this collapse into despair. The ego can be so powerful that, rather than accept that strongly held beliefs were wrong, it will produce despairing or even suicidal thoughts. There is, however, always a way out of this despair if we accept the challenge and acknowledge that a different way of living is possible. Blackthorn can help to ease the trauma of this change, and illuminate the way forward. In its white blossoms there are immense healing properties, helping us to open up to a new and totally transformed way of living.

BLADDER SENNA* *(Colutea orientalis)*

This is a very attractive bush that is covered with either yellow or tan flowers for most of the summer. Its name comes from the fact that its seed pods look like small inflated bladders. Children love to pop the immature pods. The collapsed seed pods look very much like senna pods. It is the tan-coloured flowers that are used to make the essence. This essence helps us to become free of guilt about our past. Everyone has episodes in their life that they feel ashamed about, things that they wish they had never done. The difficulty is that we look back with the wisdom of the present, something we did not have at the time that is now disturbing us. Guilt is a very destructive emotion which takes us away from the present and produces endless worries. We need to find a way of letting go of the feeling that we ought to have handled things differently, of escaping from the tyranny of severe self-judgement, and of seeing that as human beings we inevitably get things wrong from time to time, that none of us is infallible. Indeed, that is the true meaning of the word that is translated as "sin" in the Bible - to make an error, to miss the mark - as in archery. Bladder Senna helps us to get rid of the old emotional responses, to ease out of the old learned patterns of excessively harsh self-judgement. It is the flower of self-compassion and self-understanding.

Life seems to offer bizarre twists. Those who would do well to look carefully at their past behaviour rarely seem to do so. Those who do look at their past behaviour can become trapped by guilt feelings about what they did! Bladder Senna is concerned with catharsis - getting rid of things that are hindering our progress. In that, it is like our own bladder which helps us to get rid of what we no longer need. Senna pods can likewise help us get rid of waste that has been around too long for our own good! If we feel guilty, we need to get rid of the false unworthy feelings generated by an overly judgemental ego. It is here that the Bladder Senna excels, gently helping us to expel old attitudes and beliefs that have long outlived any usefulness that they may once have had for us. The Bladder Senna is a wonderful cleanser of the mind.

BLUEBELL *(Hyacinthoides non-scripta) - Component of Depression & Despair*
Bluebell is the essence to promote openness, vitality and the ability to rise above the restrictions of the past. It brings colour and fragrance after the dark winter, like the Bluebells in the woods in spring, The typical Bluebell person will be someone who has lost much of their self-esteem, dislikes themselves and feels rotten inside, the guilty "sinner" who is beyond redemption. Such people are likely to feel that everything they have worked for is somehow dying. They have become locked into negative ways of looking at themselves. Nearly always their distorted self-image has arisen from childhood conditioning where little they did met with approval. Bluebell helps to bring openness and joy where previously there was darkness and fear. It releases the spirit from old conditioned beliefs and attitudes relating to feelings of being sinful or unworthy and encourages the regrowth of self-love and self-respect. Outgrowing old negative conditionings brings us into a new and much more vital period of growth. Bluebell is about unlocking our hidden potential and bringing us into a period of personal blossoming.

BLUE PIMPERNEL* *(Anagallis arvensis var. caerulea)*
This intensely blue Pimpernel grows in the Mediterranean area. The depth of colour mirrors the deep levels of insight that this flower can stimulate. The essence relates to our ultimate goal - that of rediscovering our spiritual nature after growing up within a material world. It is inevitable that we have difficulties as we grow up. As children we are heavily influenced by everything around us, particularly the opinions and beliefs of those close to us. It is usually only after puberty that we really begin to question what we have been taught. The present "New Age" is very much about questioning the teachings and dogmas of authorities. However, there is the ever-present danger of throwing out the baby with the bath-water. We need to be able to disentangle the true teachings of the spiritual

masters from the dogmas and distortions added by those who followed afterwards. Blue Pimpernel helps us to rediscover our true roots without being dominated, and therefore restricted, by the views of any particular religion. Blue Pimpernel is the flower of spiritual truth. It helps us to discover for ourselves the true nature of our being. Because this is self-revelation, we are not enslaved by it; rather, it empowers us so that we are no longer afraid to "go out on a limb" if necessary.

BOG ASPHODEL* *(Narthecium ossifragum)*

Bog Asphodel is for the willing servants or slaves whose driving ambition is to help other people whilst ignoring their own needs. What is not understood is that help for others can only come from a natural overflowing of their own strengths and wisdom. Enthusiasm and powerful opinions are no substitute for this, and may indeed hinder rather than help. The Bog Asphodel person often finds it difficult to see that sometimes people who are suffering may need to work out their own salvation. Imposed "help" can block the true healing process, especially where the helper is influenced by their own prejudices and beliefs. Bog Asphodel people tend to be trapped by their emotional reactions to the suffering of others. They need to spend more time gently looking to their own personal growth and developing a sense of humour. A lightness of touch and a slightly whimsical approach are essential to all "healers" if they are to help others fully and not become trapped by their work. Bog Asphodel encourages people to take their missions in life more lightly and to avoid entanglements with the suffering of others. The irony is that many of the people whom they try to help may well be suffering from the same problem - that of living their lives at too great an intensity!

This is the essence of choice for all those who help others. It helps us to take life more easily and find a more relaxed (and efficient) way of working.

BRACKEN *(Alc.) (Pteridium aquilinum) (L) (A) - Component of Childhood*

Bracken Alc. is for those who habitually play the "child" role in adult life. Perhaps through parental or other domination, they were not encouraged to take increasing responsibility for their lives when they were growing up. Because of this lack of self-empowerment, they may try to assert themselves by acting the child role, being submissive yet often subversive. (Subversion is how many children get back at dominant parents.) However, playing the subservient role inevitably causes deep resentments, which, when they are not expressed openly, can lead to feelings of frustration, depression and toxic dejection. Such people are like a volcano that never erupts. Because of their inability to handle their own Fire energy, even as adults they may fill with tears when spoken to harshly. The alcoholic extract of Bracken helps to dissolve the influence of these old childish states and allow a quiet resolve to develop. The person then begins to realise that they have much more power than they had thought they had and they do not therefore need to throw their weight around to be able to assert themselves. As such people often have low self-esteem, Butterbur or the Self-Esteem composite may be very helpful when given at the same time.

BRACKEN* (Aqueous Extract) (Pteridium aquilinum) (L)

This essence relates to the blocking of psychic sensitivity in childhood. This particular difficulty is not covered by the Childhood composite. Children are naturally psychically aware from the moment of birth. However, their sensitivity often becomes blocked by others (usually adults). They may call it "childish imagination" and say that it is something that needs to be grown out of. Having imaginary playmates is just such psychic sensitivity in action. If this sensitivity is blocked by the attitudes of others, it can lead to a deep-rooted fear of the intuitive mind. It may show as a feeling that there is something wrong or unreliable about intuition. The fear of coming up-front and accepting these suppressed abilities causes problems. If the conditioning has gone very deep, then such a person can react violently against any suggestion that these faculties even exist. Their denial may be extremely vehement, even leading to accusations that such faculties are generated by the devil. Bracken people usually appear to be very "left-brain" or logical-mind-dominated, yet in fact they have great sensitivity that is well hidden. Often there is a tendency to put higher values on things than on people. Things, being predictable, fit much more comfortably into their adopted logical view of the world. Attempts to fit people into this logical view however, can cause many problems, as people inconveniently refuse to fit into a steady predictable pattern. Bracken gently helps to unblock the intuitive mind. Communication can then take place at levels other than the logical, resulting in great joy. Being involved in artistic pursuits may well help a suppressed intuitive and creative side to awaken. This in turn will encourage the left and right hemispheres of the brain to "talk to each other", promoting increased personal harmony and ease. The Yang composite essence may also be helpful in maintaining stability in the logical side, whilst forging links with the intuitive.

BUTTERBUR *(Petasites hybridus) - Component of Self-Esteem*

The Butterbur essence relates to self-esteem and personal power. Many people who are working on their own personal growth can suddenly block off at some point. This usually happens when they get a glimpse of the awesome power that is beginning to open up within themselves. If they have always shied away from power - refusing to accept their rightful place in the world - then they may be very fearful that their power will become destructive as it develops. Butterbur personalities fail to recognise their own innate goodness - the Kingdom of God within. Instead, they have the feeling that, if they go on developing their powers, they could inflict damage on other people. Lack of self-esteem and trust in themselves lies behind such difficulties. Perhaps there are childhood memories of being labelled "wicked" or "naughty". Perhaps they were not truly loved as children and so lack the self-confidence that such love brings. Perhaps they believed that they were "born in sin" or that they were "miserable sinners" (both corrupt interpretations of the original biblical texts). All of these can have a very negative effect on self-esteem. Butterbur helps to dissolve these feelings of self-distrust, revealing our innate power and spiritual birthright. Opening up to a much greater vision of the world, and one's rightful place in it, is the message of this essence.

BUTTERCUP* *(Ranunculus acris)*

This is for those who need to open up and let the sunshine into their lives. Often they have a sunny nature that has been suppressed. Because of their experiences, however, they may well have developed a negative, jaundiced view of the world. Indeed, they might have become habitual cynics, always ascribing negative motives to any good deed performed by others. These are people who have been badly treated in the past and their confidence in others has been severely shaken. Perhaps they had put their trust in someone and then had it betrayed. This flower can therefore be very helpful for the sceptic or cynic, the person who looks for ulterior motives (real or imaginary) in the actions of other people. Signs of this tendency sometimes show in such things as telling jokes that have a hidden cutting edge to them. Buttercup is for people who have lost trust in others and who need to let more light and warmth into their life. From that point of ease they can then open up to others without prejudice. The lovely Buttercup is the flower that puts us in touch with the flame of loving-kindness that lies within each of us. We can then see people as they really are, warts and all, but with love and compassion and without judgement. It is one of the flowers for the heart centre of the body.

CHARLOCK *(Sinapis arvensis) - Component of Childhood*

Growing up can be very difficult for many of us. The transition from childhood lack of responsibility to responsible adult can be very traumatic. For some it may seem easier to stay locked in the state of childhood. Like Peter Pan, they do not want to grow up. They want to live in a world of make-believe where everything is good and everything is predictable. Their naïve and trusting approach makes them prime targets for the world's con men. They need to leave behind their attachment to childish ways, but without losing the openness of the child-like way of approaching anything new. Here the essence of Charlock can be very helpful. It reveals clearly what is really going on in the world around us, rather than what we would like to believe. It helps to strip away the childhood delusions and opens up our awareness at a gentle pace. It shows us that an adult approach to life can be infinitely more rewarding than the disempowered restrictions of childhood. Charlock opens the door to being a confident, competent, joyful adult with the knowledge that accepting responsibility does not automatically imply being heavy-handed and humourless.

CHILDHOOD*

BRACKEN (Alc.) *(Pteridium aquilinum)* (L) (A), CHARLOCK *(Sinapis arvensis)*, VALERIAN *(Valeriana officinalis)*

Most, if not all of us have difficulties in life that have their roots in our childhood experiences and conditioning. They can last right through our adult lives. The difficulty is that these deeply implanted conditioned patterns can even take over our lives from time to time, depending on what triggers them. We can then behave completely out of character, afterwards having to deal with the consequence of our actions. This composite essence helps us to "come up to date" by gradually dissolving those old patterns.

Bracken helps us to escape from a habitual role of playing the subservient child, always feeling dominated by others. It works to empower us to make our own assessments in life and take responsibility for our actions.

Valerian is for those who lacked love early in life and end up playing the lost child, always seeking comfort and support from others. They are disempowered in their lives as they always are looking to please others. They do not usually know who they really are or what they really want.

Charlock is for the people who do not really want to grow up. They see adult life as threatening and want a world where everything is good and predictable. They believe that if they are good to others, everyone will be good to them. This makes them a target for all kinds of predators, including con-men. Charlock helps ease us out of those attitudes of mind so that we can discover the very real benefits of being a mature adult.

COMPACT RUSH *(Juncus conglomeratus) - Component of Sadness*
& Loneliness

Compact Rush is the remedy for sadness, for those who feel that life is passing them by. As people grow older they often become sad as they begin to dwell on what might have been: they feel that somehow they have missed out on life, that they have not been and are not being fulfilled. They begin to dwell on wasted opportunities, or opportunities that were denied them. This sadness is suppressed anger, anger that things were not different. Yet there now seems to be little that can be done. They feel disempowered and resentful. They may resent the actions of others in the past, or they may blame themselves.

Compact Rush is about new beginnings, fresh starts, about wiping the slate clean. It helps us to look on the past with compassion: that things were as they were because of the circumstances at the time, and thus it takes the sting from those past memories. Looking back is then like watching ourselves in an old movie. Neither the old emotional ties nor the emotions themselves are now there. What lies ahead is then seen as a great variety of new possibilities, possibilities that are no longer inhibited by the old resentments. Compact Rush helps us to break free of the past and so embrace the present moment with new energies and insights.

CONFUSION*

FOXGLOVE *(Digitalis purpurea),* OAK (A) *(Quercus robur),*
ROSEBAY WILLOWHERB *(Chamaenerion angustifolium),*
SOAPWORT *(Saponaria ocymoides)*

This essence is for when we feel confused and seem to have lost track of where we should be heading. When this happens our minds tend to be over active, trying to find a way out, yet continually coming up against obstacles. This composite essence helps us to relax and take a more detached view of our present difficulties.

Oak is included to counter the overactive mind, decreasing the obsessive tension that so often blocks our clarity of vision. It helps us to take a calmer view of life, to see things in a more detached way.

Rosebay Willowherb helps to keep us grounded, less likely to be blown about by every wind of change. It counters the characteristic confusion that can make us keep trying endless new things rather than settling down and looking carefully at our present surroundings.

Foxglove is for those of us who have lost our bearings and sense of direction. This can make us very despondent and cause us to lose all our fire and drive. This essence helps us to handle our difficulties more easily, freeing us from the emotional entanglements that we have built up.

Soapwort is the essence for bewilderment and confusion, that "what the hell am I doing here?" sort of feeling. This feeling often arises when we are developing spiritually and begin seeing things in a different light, but the conditioned old patterns still try to control our life. Soapwort helps us to "wash away" old outmoded ideas and concepts.

CONIFER MAZEGILL *(Gloeophyllum sepiarium)*

This essence is made from a beautiful bracket fungus that lives on dead conifer wood. It is for sudden, abrupt and irrevocable changes in life caused by personal traumas such as bereavement or divorce, or major natural disasters such as earthquakes, when the old has to die and be replaced by something new. The properties of the Conifer Mazegill essence mirror those of the fungus itself, converting the dead wood of the past into new growth of a different form. It is deeper-acting than the Shock & Trauma composite.

At such traumatic times the best form of treatment would be to start taking the Grief composite and Shock & Trauma as well as Conifer Mazegill. After the initial sting has been taken out of the situation, Conifer Mazegill should then be taken on a continuing basis, perhaps for several months. This will help to ensure that the energies of positive change are being continually activated and that we do not become trapped by old energies and memories.

CYMBIDIUM ORCHID* *(M) (Cymbidium hybridus)*

This is a lunar essence, made at the time of the full moon in our meditation room.

This essence relates to the hidden side of our nature. Its

associations are with the Yin aspect of both men and women. It is particularly concerned with the negativities that so often hide just beneath the surface of the conscious. In this area of the subconscious, close to the interface with the conscious, old resentments, anger and repression may lie hidden. Repressed feelings of any sort usually lurk close to consciousness and Cymbidium Orchid helps to bring these tensions to the surface. Once they are seen for what they really are, old shadows from the past, they lose their power over us.

It also works at much deeper levels of our subconscious. Many of us are very fearful of what we might find if we ventured into the deepest recesses of our minds. Cymbidium helps to activate the intuition (which means inner-tuition) so that we can see for ourselves that our fears have been groundless. Angels and demons are our interpretations of our visions of spirit beings. Fears of demonic forces can be very strong - as indeed can the desire to encounter angelic beings. This essence helps us to realise that these forces are merely the Yang and Yin of this dimension. Both are needed for our growth. Without the testings of Lucifer (the light-bringer) we will never know our own strengths and vulnerabilities. In the spiritual realms we are still in the area of duality, so counterbalancing forces are inevitable. Cymbidium brings insight and wisdom into our intuition so that we can see for ourselves the true nature of the spiritual dimensions of our being.

CYPRUS ROCK ROSE* (Fumana arabica)

This is for deep terrors and fears that are difficult to expose and resolve. It is more powerful and deeper-acting than the common Rock Rose used in the Bach remedies.

This yellow flower, which grows in Cyprus is for the deep terrors that we often feel unable to look at, terrors that may well disturb our dreams This essence allows us to distance ourselves from whatever is producing those terrors. We can then look at what is disturbing our lives without getting emotionally entangled with the energies involved. It is rather like letting the genie out of the bottle whilst making sure that we do not suffer as a consequence. It is very appropriate for those who are feeling suicidal, who are facing the abyss and feel that jumping into it is the only way out of their difficulties. It is for people terrified of their inner demons, those hidden forces that may dominate our lives from time to time.

It is as if this flower says, "Stop - detach yourself from all your terrors and fears and spend a little time gathering together all you have learned in this life, all your wisdom and all the positive aspects of yourself. In that insight you will discover that your hidden aspects are only fearful because they have been in the dark." The shining sunlight of the Cyprus Rock Rose brings illumination to all the dark places that have held us in states of fear or terror. This flower helps us to pause and gently take stock of our present situation. Into that pause, the energies of the flower start to create a protected environment for us restart our lives in a much more positive way.

Into that protected space come whispering voices from angelic beings with messages of love, support, learning and insight. It is rather like the story of Dick Whittington when he heard the voices saying, "Turn again Whittington - Lord Mayor of London." However deep our fears or terror, this flower can help us, even when all seems lost. At such times we may look longingly at the jump into oblivion. Yet such a view is a delusion. The human spirit does not die – it cannot die – that is an image created by our time-bound ego.

This flower dissolves the precipices of the mind, and shows instead a gentle slope leading down and forwards into a beautiful landscape covered with bright yellow flowers. Yes, we leave the past behind irrevocably, but it is to a golden future that is real, rather than an imagined cessation of all consciousness. This flower can lead us to breakthrough and a total transformation.

DELPHINIUM *(Delphinium consolida) - Component of Yin*

Delphinium is a flower that can help us to increase our powers and widen our insights. Many people who start to develop insight can get bogged down in limited perceptions, feeling that all they see is all that there is to see. It is rather like the problems faced by a Pink Purslane personality, but this time in the region of insight, rather than at the mundane level.

Selective insight can have serious repercussions, both for ourselves and for those who are using their insight to advise others. For safety we need to be able to see as wide a picture as possible. This may not be comfortable for the ego, but it is a necessary part of our personal progress.

Delphinium gently encourages us to widen our horizons, to see that there are many levels of insight and perception. It helps us to gain the courage to go beyond our previous apparently safe boundaries into (for us) uncharted regions.

On old maps they used to mark uncharted areas with such statements as "Here be Dragons", indicating their fear of what might be there. Delphinium helps us to enter the "Here be Dragons" areas of our minds without fear, knowing that all we will discover will be for our benefit.

This essence is included in the "Yin" composite because this is typically a difficulty with the Yin aspect of our nature.

DEPRESSION & DESPAIR*
BLACKTHORN *(Prunus spinosa)*, BLUEBELL *(Hyacinthoides non-scripta)*,
HAWKWEED *(Hieracium vulgatum)*,
FLOWERING CURRANT *(Ribes sanguineum)*

We all at times feel depressed when things seem to be negative and beyond our control. If we hit a really horrendous situation this can turn into despair. This essence tackles such times in several different ways.

Bluebell allows us to escape from feelings of self-dislike and self-condemnation which arise from an unrealistic self-image. It helps us to grow in new ways and, like the Bluebells in spring, find new colour and vibrancy in our life.

Hawkweed is for when we are depressed by our lack of self-confidence, our apparent inability to cope with the situation around us. We may feel that we are lost in an alien world that we cannot understand. This essence helps us to see the world with a new vision and thereby to take charge of our lives.

Flowering Currant is for those who feel that they are defeated but bravely keep carrying on against apparently impossible odds. Often such people find it hard to look directly at the situation that is giving them difficulty. This essence helps them to face up to it. Very often they can find ways of dealing with what is really there.

Blackthorn is for the depths of despair, when all seems lost with no way out of the situation - "the dark night of the soul". Blackthorn helps us in several ways. First it helps to take the sting out of our situation, lessening our anguish. Next it helps us to see how the situation arose, so that we can avoid getting into it again. Finally, it helps us to find a way out of our emotional collapse, leading us to a new and brighter future.

This essence is not intended to treat any form of clinical (i.e. chronic) depression.

DOG ROSE *(Rosa canina) - Component of Grief and Sadness & Loneliness*

The wild Dog Rose is one of the most beautiful flowers of the countryside. Its pale pink colour mirrors its properties of love and compassion - those of the "Heart protector" meridian in shiatsu and acupuncture. This is the flower that is known as Wild Rose in the Bach remedies, but ours is a sun essence which produces quite different properties from those of Bach's boiling method.

Dog Rose can help us when times are difficult, when we need loving comfort and support and when, however sympathetic our human friends may be, they cannot really help us. Often our hurt and need may have gone deep, as in bereavement, and we need something that can bring us solace and support without dulling our senses.

Dog Rose helps us by taking the sting out of hurtful situations, but at the same time its thorn may help us to remember that it also provides us with a protecting influence. Shakespeare mentioned "the slings and arrows of outrageous fortune" - that is how our life can feel at times when everything seems to be ranged against us. Here Dog Rose comes into its own, comforting, supporting and protecting us.

This flower acts in two quite distinct ways. First it gives immediate relief but it also helps us to develop our own loving and compassionate nature, and protects us from negative influences, both internal and external.

Dog Rose is for loving comfort and support. It is like having a close friend with whom we can share our difficulties and our despair. It helps us to open up to the depths of our grief and then brings the love, comfort and support that enable us to continue.

DOUBLE SNOWDROP *(Galanthus nivalis "flore-plena")*
Component of Stuck in a Rut

Double Snowdrop is for those who need to have more flexibility in their lives, who may have become frozen in their attitudes. Sometimes it is as if they have been left behind, clinging to patterns of behaviour that really belong to times past. They may have become experts in some area where nothing new is allowed to challenge their established views. Luckily most Double Snowdrop people are not so extreme; they are much more likely to have become stuck in a rut and feel unable to get out of it. Feeling old before one's time is a classic symptom of this. They need the insight to see that everything is constantly changing and that change, however uncomfortable it may feel at times, is a fact of life. It is fear of change that is the main Double Snowdrop characteristic. Often this fear results in heavy, serious feelings. This essence encourages a lightness of touch and a rejoicing in the newness of life. They can not only see then that nothing is the same from moment to moment, but they can rejoice that it is so. Double Snowdrop helps to break up the crusts of rigid attitudes that are keeping out joy and freedom, and to build trust and a sense of security through the period of transformation.

DWARF PURPLE VETCH* *(Vicia villosa ssp. eriocarpa)*

This flower comes from the mountains of Cyprus and grows in very rocky conditions on the mountains. The essence is for very old patterns established in childhood, particularly where relationships and sexual attitudes are concerned. It works at a deeper level than Tufted Vetch and is more suitable for intransigent problems, especially for those that arise in puberty.

At puberty changing power and sexual roles often produce anguish and uncertainty, of impotence in handling the sexual games that are played out by both boys and girls. Understanding of the opposite sex is often blocked, yet a desire to relate to them is often stifled by the fear of being ridiculed. This can open relationships with the opposite sex impossible, the idea of having a heterosexual sexual relationship even revolting.

The Dwarf Purple Vetch helps to free us from the intimidating ghosts of the past that "have us in their thrall". It enables us to understand how we became enslaved in the first place and offers us the key to the door of true personal and sexual freedom - freedom from guilt.

EARLY PURPLE ORCHID* *(Orchis mascula)*

This essence is concerned with helping us to get in touch with our true nature. It can be particularly helpful when old patterns are falling away and the new ways of being have not become firmly established. At these times we can feel weakened by a loss of personal identity. It is then that we are vulnerable and can easily fall back into the negativity of outmoded ways, just because they are familiar. Often we may prefer to polish the bars of our cage rather than fly away through the open cage door! Early Purple Orchid begins to dissolve the blocks which are impeding our progress, whilst bringing harmony to the mind-body-spirit. It helps to open the channels of communication within us, including blocked chakras. Because these blocked areas distort our main energy flows, they can and do affect our lives. Often we may be quite unaware of these patterns asserting themselves. Sometimes this essence can greatly assist the action of another, more specific, essence. For example, Milk Thistle, for a blocked-off ability to love, is enhanced by Early Purple Orchid. Similarly, it can be very helpful to use it with the Transition composite, when someone is having difficulty in allowing new energies into their life.

FEARS*

BETONY *(Stachys officinalis)*, MAHONIA *(Mahonia aquifolium)*, GREATER CELANDINE *(Chelidonium majus)*

Fears can inhibit so much of our lives and can often be difficult to eradicate. They deny us much of our freedom and enjoyment of life. The intention behind this essence is to bring our fears out into the open where they can be seen for what they really are - "paper tigers" that looked ferocious when hidden in dark corners but in fact have no real power or substance. Deeply rooted fears can date back to childhood and so the Childhood essence can often help when given at the same time.

Betony is for unrecognisable fears, fears that can make us feel unloved, unwanted or unworthy. In extreme cases they can drive people to contemplate suicide. Betony helps us to see that such fears are groundless by shedding light in the dark places of the mind. In so doing it helps us to discover that inner treasure-house of the intuitive mind which all too often we have lost touch with.

Mahonia helps to free us from the fear of our own inner power. Such fear usually arises from seeing the immense damage that can be caused by fanatical people. Yet those who fear their own power are those who are the most trustworthy, the least likely to misuse that personal power. Mahonia brings the fragrance of the divine into our life, empowering whatever we need to be doing.

Greater Celandine is for those who fear their spiritual dimension - the core of their being. They have unwittingly set up a barrier between themselves and the source of their existence. This can produce a whole variety of fears including a deep-rooted fear of death and a rejection of the possibility of anything other than the physical. Greater Celandine gradually helps to dissolve those barriers, bringing ease and realignment of the mind-body-spirit unity.

FIRETHORN *(F) (Pyrancantha atalantioides) - Component of Anger & Frustration*

Firethorn is the essence for helping us to balance our energies. Many people with unstable energies have problems arising from suppressed emotions. A typical Firethorn pattern is where suppressed emotions (often caused by old conditionings) build up and stay hidden until they finally explode. After this violent release of energy has taken place, people often panic and retreat within themselves. This can lead to an alternating energy pattern of blowing hot and cold, making life very difficult for others. Firethorn people may also be over-emotionally involved in what they do: they may become very possessive about their work or expect everyone else to live up to excessively high standards. The energy needs to be appropriate for the matter in hand, not too little and not too much. Firethorn helps to bring balance and a more mature attitude to handling life so that the energies can ebb and flow as they are needed. The result is greater tranquillity and ease. Once the energies have stabilised, the underlying cause or causes of the instability can usually be seen. From here it is much easier to see how to deal with them, though in many cases we find that they have already been resolved!

FLOWERING CURRANT *(Ribes sanguineum) - Component of Depression & Despair*
Flowering Currant is for those who feel that they are facing inevitable defeat in some part of their life. They have largely lost heart but they still have the energy and courage to keep on going. The emotional pressure will have made them feel twisted and collapsed, yet they still try to protect the spark that keeps them going. Indeed, their physical bodies may have twisted in response to the mental pressures. The real problem with people in this state is that they do not recognise their own strength and the power of their insight. They find it difficult to look directly at what opposes them. Often they are so frightened or intimidated that, like children, they try to hide their faces, hoping it will all go away. Flowering Currant helps with the discovery of personal power, thereby bringing the confidence to face up to opposition. It is only by fearlessly looking directly at opposing forces that we can see how to deflect or overcome them. Even when things are not so extreme, Flowering Currant can be very helpful. It encourages us to let go of fears and to open up to the reality of our present situation.

FORSYTHIA *(Oleacea intermedia) - Component of Unification*
Forsythia allows us open up to our spiritual nature, bringing joy and a sense of freedom in that realisation. Forsythia essence is complex as it covers a set of inter related properties.
First of all it helps us to get rid of old outgrown ideas and concepts that would otherwise get in the way of our further development. It is

as if it squeezes us through a narrow tube, expelling anything that we no longer need. Such an experience is not at all pleasant, yet it may be necessary for our further growth and development.

Second it encourages us to open up to the spiritual reality which our logical left brain may have been steadily opposing. Our logical nature likes to be in control, and in the realm of the spiritual it has to take a back seat to our intuitive side. This obviously generates fears and anxieties that Forsythia can reduce.

Finally we learn to appreciate that there are many different realities in the spiritual dimension. This prevents us from developing a narrow dogmatic viewpoint where once again the logical mind tries to take over and so become a self-styled "expert" in spiritual matters.

Through Forsythia we can keep an open and non-dogmatic mind.

FOXGLOVE *(Digitalispurpurea) - Component of Confusion*

Foxglove is the essence for people who have lost their bearings and their sense of direction. They can become very despondent and lose all their drive. They know that somewhere there is a way out of their difficulties, but somehow they just cannot find it. They try to push through ways that are blocked to them, with all the consequent frustration. Often there is a clear way out of their difficulties but they are too emotionally blocked to see it. People who are continually seeking new therapies for their ailments may well fall into this category. They are often too intellectual about their difficulties - trying to think their way out of their problems. The resulting mental exertion makes things even more confused and woolly.

Foxglove reduces our emotional entanglement with difficulties, thereby creating distance from the "problems". With the resulting quieter mind, new ways of looking at things will emerge, the confusion and bewilderment naturally receding. The answers that are needed will then reveal themselves with such clarity that there will be little doubt as to their accuracy.

FUJI CHERRY *(Prunus incisa) - Component of Tranquillity*

Fuji Cherry is the key essence for developing a calm and quiet mind. There is a close link between mind and body tensions. A tense mind creates a tense body and the resulting pattern of body tensions will reinforce this tense attitude. We need something that will help the mind to quieten whilst preventing the body tensions from pushing us back into the tense mind situation.

Fuji Cherry encourages the mind to relax, bringing in a sense of calm and detachment to replace previous worries and difficulties. As the emotional temperature is reduced, so are the stresses on the body, in turn reducing the reinforcing stresses on the mind. This enables us to see the problems that have stressed us in a calmer and more detached light which allows us to see how to adjust our life so that we are no longer dominated by the situations around us.

Fuji Cherry is invaluable in helping us to detach from the rat race of the mind, and if necessary may also help us to detach ourselves from the physical rat races that might be causing us so much distress. This is the key essence for developing a quiet reflective mind.

GREATER CELANDINE *(Chelidonium majus) - Component of Fears*

Greater Celandine is for those who fear their spiritual nature. Many of us have put up, however unwittingly, a mental block between ourselves and the source of our existence. Often this is because the logical mind, once more, does not want to accept dimensions of reality that it cannot understand, and over which it has no control. This fear of the non-physical can produce many different problems. There may be a deep-rooted fear of death, or fears of anything to do with the psychic dimensions of life. Fears of this sort may reveal themselves in the form of tangled, tortured personalities. These people may be bitter and self-hating, or they may feel that they have a mission in life to preach the philosophy of materialism. Perhaps they see themselves as enlightened persons who expose as fraud, those people, however genuine, who have conflicting views.

This essence has the property of gradually dissolving the inner barriers that have been erected between the left and right hemispheres of the brain. As these dissolve, the intuitive mind can take its rightful place as part of a composite whole. Then there will be nothing to oppose the establishment of a way of life that will support all aspects of body and mind. It is from this secure base that inner illumination will grow, bringing about a new and total realignment of the body-mind-spirit unity.

GRIEF*

SHEEP'S SORREL *(Rumex acetocella)*, DOG ROSE *(Rosa canina)*, YORKSHIRE FOG *(Holcus lanathus)*, TRAILING ST. JOHN'S WORT *(Hypericum humifusum)*

This composite is for people suffering from bereavement or the loss of something precious in their lives. At such times we need to be able to express our grief so that it does not become locked within us.

Yorkshire Fog (a moorland grass) encourages us to shed our tears and symbolically wash away the anguish that naturally occurs at such times.

Sheep's Sorrel helps us leave bitterness behind, the resentment caused by feeling "why should this have happened to me?" We can then accept what has happened so that we do not become trapped by bitter feelings.

Trailing S. John's Wort is for healing. It takes the sting out of the situation and reduces the emotional tension and desperation that are so often a part of the grieving process.

Dog Rose is for loving comfort and support when we feel totally bereft, and other people, however caring, may seem very distant. It also allows us to open up to the depths of our grief without fear.

HAIRY SEDGE* *(Carex hirta)*

This essence is for those who find difficulty in living in the present and who tend to dwell either in the past or in possible futures. This lack of present-moment awareness often causes difficulty with short-term memory. Such people can be brought into the present moment, perhaps by something that has an impact on their personal well-being, or something that brings them pleasure, which will normally be remembered. However, things that seem less important will most likely be forgotten as their attention is not wholly engaged by what is happening around them. Sometimes poor memory can be due to fear. There may be a reluctance to see what is really there because of the threat that such awareness could bring to their beliefs. This causes memory to be selective, reinforcing personal attitudes and opinions.

Anything which would be threatening to those beliefs will then be ignored and forgotten.

If people are too entrenched in their beliefs, it might be better to start with the Stuck in a Rut composite. Alternatively, both essences could be given together. How much progress can be made with such clients will largely depend upon their willingness to take part in the whole healing process.

HAWKWEED *(Hieracium vulgatum) - Component of Depression & Despair*

Hawkweed is for the type of despair caused by a lack of self-confidence. This is not the Blackthorn pit, but more a feeling of having lost touch with one's original roots. There may be a feeling of being lost in a hellish alien world. Those with some religious beliefs could well feel that they have been damned and are now beyond redemption. In this state there is a sense of being a victim. Such pressures can cause a split in the psyche and an abrupt personality change. Hawkweed helps us to ease out of these depressive emotional states, allowing us to feel more at home in the world in which we live. In many ways it invites us to be reborn, with a greater sense of balance and wisdom.

HEATH BEDSTRAW *(Galium saxatile) - Component of Tranquillity*

Heath Bedstraw supports us as we let go of our tensions and find new and better ways of living. Personal change is usually challenging as many of our concepts and beliefs are put to the test and often found to be wanting. Needless to say, the stresses so caused may be enough to make us want to go back to our previous way of living - stressful though it may have been. This is a problem that many people who embark on a spiritual path find difficulty with - how to change their way of being without feeling overwhelmed by it.

Heath Bedstraw, as its name suggests, grows on moors and fells and similar wild places. The essence made from the tiny white flower helps to underpin and support us as we change. We are used to our habitual tensions with their consequent anxieties. As we embark on a new path in life we can feel very vulnerable as our circumstances change. Strangely enough, this can be due to either new stresses or a reduction in stress. Either way we can feel threatened and disoriented. Heath Bedstraw helps us to relax and supports us in such times of major change in our life. It is often very helpful when given as a support to other essences that are actively promoting change.

HIMALAYAN BLUE POPPY* *(Meconopsis betonicifolia)*

This essence is to help us recognise the talents that we brought with us into the world and then to develop them for our personal fulfilment. We are not blank slates that the world then writes upon. Each of us comes with different characteristics, many of which could be genetic or from previous lifetimes. These characteristics are our spiritual heritage and for some may well be related to a lineage in a particular form of spiritual training. If we are to fulfil our potential in this lifetime, then it will be important that we build on strengths gained in the past. This does not mean that we will become Zen monks if that was our pattern for a previous life. Rather we will need to build on the experiences gained during those times.

This essence relates to our spiritual quest and enables us to have a much wider perspective on the multi-dimensional world that we find ourselves in. For anyone wishing to develop their insight and psychic skills, this is the essence of choice. It also enables us to communicate with other kingdoms, plant, animal or mineral, by stimulating our intuition.

This is the essence for the spiritual warrior, the person dedicated to being "valiant for Truth". The more we can understand about this wonderful universe and about our own purpose in life, the more fulfilled we will become and the more we will be able to help others.

HOLLY LEAF *(Ilex aquifolium) (L) (A) Component of Anger & Frustration*

Holly Leaf is the key remedy for anger and resentment - it mirrors our difficulties in its sharp defensive prickles.

There are two different forms of anger. The first is a natural, healthy reaction to unreasonable provocation. In this case, after the initial flash of anger, we are able to deal skilfully with the situation that caused the emotion. However, if for any reason we are unable to deal with the anger as it arises, it will be held within the mind and body and emerge as resentment. It is this retained anger that causes our difficulties.

Holly Leaf essence acts in several ways. First, it acts as a protection so that we do not rise to the bait so readily. This helps us not to react instantaneously to provocation. It empowers us by giving a breathing space before we act on the situation that made us angry. Second, it takes the sting out of the situation by deflecting any intended desire to hurt us. Like the watery shine on the holly leaf which prevents things sticking to it, the essence enables us to be less sensitive to the antagonism of others. In addition, the sharp spines of the Holly can remind us that the essence of Holly Leaf can act as a protection, showing others that it is not wise to provoke us as they may well be hurt themselves.

HONESTY *(Lunaria annua) Component of Yin*

This is for a lack of openness and receptivity. This can occur when the Yin (right brain) aspect of a person is active, but in a negative way. If the assertive Yang side has been suppressed, perhaps because of a dominant parent, then that person may use the feminine Yin side of their nature in an attempt to assert themselves. The difficulty is that the Yin aspect of the personality cannot be used to mimic the Yang. The result is that the person then attempts to control situations by subversion. This "negative female" is typically secretive, not telling the whole story about things, and thus maintaining a hold on the situation. This characteristic is due to a failure to grow up - maintaining the "deceitful child" who resorts to deceit because that is the only way they can assert themselves. Honesty helps us to overcome the need for these subterfuges. Reducing emotional dependency on negative female ways encourages openness and honesty. At the same time a calm Yang "masculine" energy will develop to protect the otherwise vulnerable new state of being.

HONEYSUCKLE *(Lonicera periclymenum) - Component of Sadness & Loneliness*

The wild yellow Honeysuckle growing in our hedgerows possesses very strong healing properties. It has an exquisite scent which is strongest in the late evening. This essence is included in the Sadness composite to encourage us to make our fragrance known to others. Sadness and loneliness isolate us from other people. We turn inwards and become increasingly closed to the positive aspects of the world around us. Honeysuckle encourages change at a subtle level, so we become more approachable to others. The barriers to the outside world that we erect during periods of sadness and loneliness are natural, but unfortunately are often very counter-productive. All too often we fail to appreciate just how withdrawn we may appear to other people. Honeysuckle helps ease the pain in the heart, enabling us to open up to the world around us. Through this opening up, loving help will often flow in our direction because we then appear far less defensive.

Honeysuckle has three properties in particular that make it a key part of the Sadness remedy. First, it brings ease and comfort to our heart, reinforcing the action of Dog Rose. Second, it helps us to pull down over-protective barriers that we may have erected between ourselves and the world around us. Finally, like the fragrant Honeysuckle, our own fragrance will be carried out into the world and those positive qualities will attract love and healing towards us.

INDIAN BALSAM *(Impatiens glandulifera)* - Component of Obsession

Indian Balsam brings quietness and healing to minds that are disturbed, helping us to distance ourselves from thoughts that are causing distress.

There can be little more distressing than a mind caught up in endless mind-loops that just will not stop. Under such circumstances there can be no peace because, as soon as the mind starts to quieten, new looping thoughts arise.

Indian Balsam prevents such thoughts from reinforcing themselves by reducing the emotional tensions in the mind. We take our thoughts less seriously and do not pay them so much attention. It helps the mind to steady down to a point where we can once more take charge of our thinking, rather than feeling that we have got on a strange merry-go-round that just will not stop.

Indian Balsam likes to grow by rivers and it may help us, when taking the essence, to feel that we are once more sitting on a quiet river bank, just watching the wildlife and the ripples on the water. This essence helps us to just be, quietly observing the world around us. It can be very helpful to take the composite essence of Tranquillity at the same time.

IVY *(Hedera helix) - Component of Shock & Trauma*

This essence is to help ground us in situations where shock might otherwise make us space out and even lose the will to live.

There are times for everyone when life can feel just not worth living. It may be "the slings and arrows of outrageous fortune" when everything we touch seems to crumble to dust and disaster. It may be that the shock of a bad accident has made us lose touch with reality. Either way the desire to keep on living can desert us and all we want is a cessation of our troubles. In such circumstances we need an essence that will help to root us back in the physical world, to feel secure and loved. This is where Ivy can help.

Ivy mirrors the properties that we are looking for in such circumstances. It can awaken in us its powers of toughness, resilience and power. Ivy is a survivor! If we embrace its powers, it will not willingly let us escape into illness or even death.

LARCH *(Larix decidua) - Component of Yin*

This essence is for awakening the true power of Yin within us - the power of the intuitive and the receptive.

In Eastern terms, Yin represents many things. It is the shadow side of a mountain, the depths rather than the heights. It is the receptive side of our nature - the intuitive. It is about love, compassion and nurturing. It is soft but powerful in its softness. In many ways it is femininity in its purest form - yet it is far more than that. Yin accepts rather than confronts. Yin wisdom is far deeper than the logical Yang ideas of truth.

This essence helps us to develop our Yin aspects so that they can balance the Yang side of our being. Many men, as well as some women, have deep troubles with this aspect of their personality. Yang likes to be in charge, to go out there and do things. Men tend to be

Yang-dominant and because Yang fears the wisdom of Yin, it tends to dominate Yin. It covers this up by pretending that intuition (which means inner tuition) is just wishful thinking.

The essence of Larch (made from the red male catkins in the spring) is a powerful activator of Yin qualities. It strengthens the Yin side so that the intuition can be heard when it is wiser than the logical side of our nature. It would be wise to take a look at the Yin composite details as well because at times it may be that the wider aspects of the composite essence would be more appropriate.

LEOPARDSBANE* *(Doronicum pardalianches)*

This is the essence for those who are awakening to their true selves, whether consciously or not. They may feel that they are living on a knife-edge and indeed may begin to believe that they are going mad. Such feelings can be very distressing. Yet they can be a very positive sign, indicating the beginning of a way through the veils of conditioned thought. The negative aspect of the Leopardsbane characteristic is that it can lead to serious depression and even to suicidal thoughts. Because of the powerful emotions generated in such states, there is often a real problem with addiction to the feelings of negativity. Leopardsbane is useful in two ways: first, in lessening the attachment to emotional extremes; second, in allowing the perceptions to broaden. The people who suffer in this way are often very perceptive and may be seeing something of the nature of the "madness" of mankind - the madness of clinging to beliefs or situations that can only cause pain and suffering. They need to see beyond that pain and suffering. They may then reach a point where they can understand that this madness is an inevitable part of life, at least until people begin to awaken and change. Leopardsbane helps them to see their own sufferings, as well as those of others, with understanding and compassion.

LESSER STITCHWORT *(Stellaria graminea) - Component of Liberation*

Lesser Stitchwort is the essence for those who need to escape from the thought patterns and influences that possess them. The things that possess us can be many and various: they may be attitudes and opinions that we have come to believe in; or someone may be trying to dominate us; or perhaps we have become so involved with our own possessions that in reality they now possess us, as we endeavour to hold on to them. We need to reduce our dependency on things and relationships. When that happens, what we truly need will naturally stay with us and the rest will fall away. Lesser Stitchwort works in two ways. First, it helps to dissolve our emotional entanglement with objects, events and people. These greatly restrict our freedom of action. Second, it acts, like a guiding star, to illuminate the path ahead. It also give us the insight and encouragement to follow that path as it opens up before us.

LIBERATION*
LESSER STITCHWORT *(Stellaria graminea)*, SCARLET PIMPERNEL *(Anagallis arvensis)*, WILD MALLOW *(Malva sylvestris)*

This essence is for those who have become trapped by their circumstances. It may be that there is a dominant friend or partner who is causing the difficulties. They do not feel in charge of their own lives.

Lesser Stitchwort helps us disentangle ourselves from our difficulties. It can then act as a guiding star, showing us clearly the path ahead that we need to be following.

Scarlet Pimpernel is for those who are either obsessed or possessed by another person. In either situation a mutual dependency tends to build up. This essence empowers us so that we can ease ourselves out of the situation without it being too obvious to the other person.

Wild Mallow helps bring the possessive links to the surface where we can see them for what they are. Seeing the true nature of the forces that have enslaved us can be very enlightening and in that revelation those forces lose their hold over us.

LICHEN *(Marchantia polymorpha L.) – Component of Protection & Clearing*
Lichens are strange plants composed of two different species living together in an interlocked relationship. The essence of Lichen mirrors this but in a rather different manner. We are part of the universe and the universe is a part of us, but when that relationship becomes strained, when we feel alienated from the source of our being, life can

be very difficult and unrewarding. Indeed, in extreme circumstances we may feel that there is just no point in going on living.

Lichen enables us to bond firmly once more with the universe and all that it contains, not only at the material level of physical earth, but also at the psychic and spiritual levels - all part of our birthright.

This is not always an easy essence to take, as it may be uncomfortable for us to realise just how much we are a part of everything. Love is not always an easy thing so far as our ego is concerned, yet it is vital for our well-being and development. It is broad-reaching love that is carried in the messages of Lichen.

LILAC* *(Syringa vulgaris "Massena")*

This is for those who have failed to develop fully and blossom in their life and whose personal growth has therefore been stunted. They may feel shrivelled up, which may sometimes be echoed in a shrivelled or stunted physical appearance. This may have been caused by a dominant parent, partner or teacher. The result of such domination is an inability to express freely what is felt. Lilac encourages an opening up and a restart into growth. We realise that all is not lost, that we have simply been hibernating. Unblocking locked-in energies can give remarkably rapid personal growth, rather like plant growth in the spring. Often Lilac people have difficulty in accepting their own worth and potential. Indeed, they may have become addicted to being victims, feeling safe in their prison. Opening the door of the cage and looking out into a much wider world can feel pretty threatening. Love and support are needed to help them through such a major change. We are talking here about true love, not sentimentality - support, not indulgence.

It is often advisable to give Bistort at the same time as this will give the added support needed through such a period of major change. Equally, Magnolia or Wild Rose could be considered for reinforcing the love that is needed.

LILY OF THE VALLEY* *(Convallaria majalis)*

This is the essence for yearning, for those who desire things that are unattainable. Perhaps they are in love with someone and those feelings are not returned. Perhaps they yearn to experience contact with the "spiritual" planes and the search has proved fruitless. It is like searching for the Holy Grail and never finding it, however hard we try. Behind the yearning there is a sense of desperation and of being incomplete until the object of desire is achieved. It is like a heart burn that will not go away. The answer lies in giving up the search! Things will then begin to resolve themselves. Emotional searching only blocks the process. In effect, things have been seen back-to-front. It has been likened to playing hide-and-seek with Truth. Lily of the Valley helps to create "the empty cup" so that what we truly need can find the space within us and enter in. It is about learning to trust the forces that created us in the first place.

MAGNOLIA* *(Magnolia x loebneri "Leonard Messel")*

This Magnolia essence is concerned with our heart centre. It is associated with the double-edged sword of love and compassion. Unconditional love is not necessarily pleasant; it has nothing of the sentimental aspects that so often pass for love. Indeed, it can be very disturbing to be on the receiving end of its attentions! It will not let us go, however much we try to avoid it. The Magnolia essence mirrors that love: like a bird it soars, knowing no boundaries, only vast open spaces with infinite possibilities. It relates to deep meditation states where the ego self no longer exists. The power and possibilities of such love are awe-inspiring.

The message of Magnolia is simple. Surrender to love. Surrender to your own inner wisdom which knows no limits. Accept that battles will result from the rearguard action of old beliefs, but remember that these battles are for your own personal freedom. Magnolia shows that true love does, indeed, conquer all. It allows us to let go of our shadow existence and grasp the nettle of reality. Magnolia helps us to go forward into those expanded realms with courage and fortitude. It mirrors man's deep desire for new and superior ways of living. It presents us with challenges, but also with the ways of meeting those challenges.

MAHONIA *(Mahonia aquifolium)* - Component of Fears

Mahonia helps to free us from the fear of our negative potential.

Many people feel that deep within themselves they are basically "evil", often because they were told they were naughty or disobedient when they were children. Or because some religions maintain that mankind is inherently evil - quoting Genesis or the concept of original sin. Freud built on these fears, adding sexuality to them for good measure! This is not my experience of life. I now accept that our problems stem from such acquired characteristics as greed, rather than from an inherently fatally flawed nature.

Mahonia can help us by bringing the fragrance of the divine into our lives, enabling us to see that it is our fears that inhibit our spiritual progression - not a supposed "evil" within us. It shows us that our fears are largely fictitious, products of conditioning and imagination. When the burden of fear lifts, there is a great release of the energy which has been trapped by the negative thoughts. That energy will then activate unconditional love within the Heart Chakra, love that has been blocked by the fears of the past. This is a very uplifting essence that can be a great help to all those who feel that they are inadequate, that there is a hidden "dead hand" that holds them back from discovering the beauty that lies hidden within them.

MARIGOLD *(Calendula officinalis) - Component of Yin*

This is the essence for the person who has largely blocked their Yin sensitivity. Whereas the Aqueous Bracken personality is merely suppressing their sensitivity, the Marigold personality has gone one stage further. They may vehemently deny and attack any suggestion that there is anything in this universe other than what can be scientifically detected and explained. The extreme of this characteristic is the professional sceptic who seeks to expose fake healers, mediums, dowsers, etc. Often these people are inherently sensitive but are afraid to admit it. As Shakespeare put it "Methinks he doth protest too much". They could well find it too threatening to embrace fully the feminine Yin side of their nature.

Marigold is therefore particularly useful for all those who have largely blocked the light from their feminine side. It helps to dissipate the fear of the feminine aspects and gently encourages the growth of positive insight. Sometimes this essence is indicated where a person seems to be well-balanced so far as their intuitive side is concerned. In this case it may be that their intuitive potential is much greater than they have so far been able to accept.

MARSH THISTLE *(Cirsium palustre) - Component of Stuck in a Rut*

Marsh Thistle is for those who have become locked in the past – a common experience. The familiar and routine are relied upon for support and anything very new is met with fear and suspicion. When this attitude becomes chronic, it can be a difficult one to change. Marsh Thistle helps the fear of newness to fade but allows the change to take place gently. Unless the approach is gentle, when the views are entrenched, either the old fears could re-assert themselves or the opposite could happen. In this case everything new is welcomed, however inappropriate it may be. Once the fixed viewpoints have disappeared, then what was previously seen as a haven from the threats of the world will be seen as it really was - a cage, a prison whose door was locked. Marsh Thistle is the remedy for all those who are trapped in routine attitudes and situations. It is about being open to newness and change and welcoming those changes as they occur.

MEADOW RUE* *(Phalictrum dipterocarpum)*

The Chinese Lesser Meadow Rue is the essence for discernment, showing us what will be to our detriment and what will be to our benefit. It is a tall plant but very fine and graceful. Its leaves are similar to those of the maidenhair fern. The flowers are small but incredibly beautiful, the petals a violet-purple with striking creamy-white anthers and stamens. This is the flower of service to others. Yet this is not the message of self-sacrifice - far from it. The message of Meadow Rue is to put aside greed and self-seeking because those are the weapons that not only destroy us personally, but that could ultimately destroy mankind. It was perhaps not without reason that this flower came to my attention after some notable corporate scandals. They showed all too clearly how greed can have a catastrophic effect on others. Whether corporate or personal greed, the end result is the same.

Meadow Rue shows us how to discriminate between the desires

that are healthy for us and those which carry the seeds of destruction within them. It is the flower of equanimity - of balance. It enables us to live with grace, poise and ease in a difficult world. Discernment carries with it the message of service to others, the realisation that no man is an island and that we all need to co-operate for the general good. Meadow Rue co-operates well with the Bladder Senna in helping those who feel guilty. Bladder Senna helps old negative feelings to fall away, while Lesser Meadow Rue brings in discernment, so that we can choose well what direction to take with the newly released energies.

MEDITERRANEAN SAGE* *(Salvia fruticosa)*

This essence represents all that is powerful within the element of Earth. It mirrors the energy and wisdom of the Earth Mother. It helps us to become firmly rooted in the material world. Such "earthing" is vital if we are to raise our consciousness to other levels of perception.

Mediterranean Sage has deep roots and it brings to us that same quality of steadfastness and dependability. It manages to grow where there seems to be little to nourish it. It thus has very close links with the earth and its inner wisdom. Sage has always been linked with wisdom, but the flower essence made from plants growing in wild mountainous areas has additional qualities. This essence brings warmth and comfort as well as quiet wisdom.

Wisdom arises from an interaction between insight and experience. Experience is vital: without it, insight is just information that may or may not be correct. True wisdom is that which has been proved (i.e. tested) in the "furnace of adversity" of life. Deep within us there is a legacy of this wisdom which can be awakened. Sage can catalyse and speed up this process. The insights it brings can awaken deep inner strengths so that we can remain unmoved and at peace, even through major traumas.

Sage essence also reflects the quality of stillness. The Earth element is very still, acting as a firm base for the other elements. Sage can help us to mirror this stillness within our own beings, so that we can safely venture into other realms of reality. It acts as a stable yet shimmering interface between different levels of consciousness.

MILK THISTLE* *(Sonchus oleraceus)*

This essence relates to the chest area of the body - in Eastern terms the heart centre (Heart Chakra). For many people this is a vulnerable place because it is where they experience fear as well as love. In many ways love and fear are opposites. Fear can suppress love, yet love can overcome fear. Difficulties in this part of the body are often due to blocked-off love of the self and of other people. Typical physical symptoms are a "caved-in" look where the shoulders are pulled forwards and downwards and the breathing is restricted by a pinched-in chest. In such cases it can be very helpful to work with suitable exercises, designed to ease the shoulders back and help the chest-box to expand forwards, outwards and upwards. The "defeated" posture is a fairly sure sign of people who have a poor opinion of themselves - self-love and self-esteem are at a very low level. The patterns may well have been established in early childhood when there has been a perceived lack of close love from the mother. Milk Thistle encourages people to open up to love and let go of the fears that are restricting them. In opening at this level, there may be temporary feelings of pain or increased vulnerability. This is due to positive change taking place. Reassurance and loving help may be needed until sufficient courage has been gained to look the world straight in the face. They will then begin to understand that the world itself is, in reality, a loving environment. A very useful and powerful essence, Milk Thistle is about helping people to bring more light and love into their lives. Early Purple Orchid assists the process when given at the same time.

MONK'S HOOD* *(Aconitum napellus)*

This is for long-standing difficulties, the roots of which lie in the past - very often in childhood. Such chronic difficulties show that problems have been carried forward rather than being resolved at the time when they originally occurred. Very often Monk's Hood people have not updated their views of the world, and have retained their old attitudes and beliefs. In childhood they could well have been heavily indoctrinated with the ideals and dogmas of religion, politics or nationalism. As a result they are often dogmatic in areas of belief.

They need to be able to understand just how they were indoctrinated in those early years. Monk's Hood gently helps them to see things of the past as they really were - with all the old attitudes and emotions stripped away and with the wisdom of the present but also with compassionate understanding. Through seeing parents and other dominant influences in far less black and white terms, they are freed from the past.

MOSS *(Discranella heteromalla) (P) (A) - Component of Self-Esteem*

Moss is the essence for those who fear the dark spaces within themselves. As with the childhood fears of darkness, many people fear the uncharted areas within their own beings. For some, these fears may have been instilled in childhood by such teachings as the inherently sinful nature of humanity. For others it may be the feeling of having dark murky secrets hidden within the subconscious mind. There are many people who struggle on, dogged by these deep fears. Sometimes they feel compelled to help others in a desperate attempt to atone for the "evil" that they feel within themselves. Moss helps to show that fears about the subconscious are only paper tigers - shadows that disappear when light is shed on them. It is fear that prevents the light of insight from entering the mind, and fear is therefore responsible for the dark spaces. Moss lessens these addictive fears and loosens up the constrictions. The dark spaces are then transformed into places of light and illumination.

NASTURTIUM *(Tropaeolum majus) - Component of Yang*

This is for those who know that they need to make changes in their lives. Although they may wish to do so, they feel unable to start the change process. There are two factors needed for this to happen and Nasturtium helps with both of them. The first is having sufficient energy to initiate the change. The second is a recognition of the need to let go of the attitudes and fears that will otherwise inhibit the change process. In fact it is usually this latter factor that is the key problem. Some people experience guilt feelings or fears about changes in personality. Others will be afraid of having to come up-front and accept a more responsible role in life. Nasturtium helps us to accept different roles, to accept the challenge of change and to view such change positively rather than with fear or dread. Nasturtium encourages change, growth and a bright new future.

NORWAY MAPLE *(Acer platanoides) - Component of Unification*

Norway Maple helps us to understand more about our true nature by freeing up our minds so that we can more easily enter other levels of consciousness.

We are all multi-dimensional beings - much more complex that we are normally prepared to admit. Many people just stay with their consciousness firmly in the Earth plane. This is ultimately unsatisfactory: not only do they fear the apparent end caused by death, but they also fail to discover the riches revealed by exploring other dimensions.

Norway Maple works to free up our consciousness so that we no longer put blocks on what we are prepared to accept when we enter states of meditation and insight. This reluctance is not so much caused by fear in this case, but rather the feeling that we are content with the extent of our present explorations.

Norway Maple entices us to develop an enquiring mind. It encourages us to go further and deeper in just the same way as a good meditation teacher will stretch us so that we do not settle into a lethargic or complacent state. Norway Maple facilitates movement between different levels of consciousness so that whenever we need information it can be made available to us with ease and accuracy.

OAK (A) *(Quercus robur) - Component of Confusion*

This is of great help where there is confusion, an over-active mind, or a lack of inner strength.

When we feel buffeted about by the world we can easily feel confused, lacking the courage of our own convictions. Under these circumstances the quality we need is that of being rooted, yet maintaining a broad overview of what is going on. This is the quality of Wood in the Chinese Five Elements. It is therefore not surprising that it is the flowers of the English Oak that are so appropriate for treating this condition.

Oak helps us to feel at home in the world whilst maintaining a quiet overview of what is going on around us. It supports us in developing a quiet inner strength so that, like the oak tree, we will not easily be overturned by opposing forces. We become strong and resilient.

From this strong viewpoint we can then watch the world with quiet amusement, seeing, perhaps in amazement, just how seriously many people take themselves. It teaches us not to react against the world, but to act with freedom on the circumstances around us. We are then no longer imprisoned by old reaction patterns that can so often disempower us.

OBSESSION*

INDIAN BALSAM *(Impatiens glandulifera)*, RAGWORT *(Senecio jacobaea)*, WHITE DEAD NETTLE *(Lamium album)*

This essence is for those who have become locked in endless looping thoughts.

Indian Balsam is included to help reduce the mental energy levels that are driving the thoughts round and round. It helps to quieten the mind and so reduce the tendency for the thoughts to keep on running in the same obsessive pattern.

Ragwort is the key essence in breaking the loops of thought, enabling us to see the futility of such thought, whilst empowering us to break the self-sustaining problem.

White Dead Nettle is included for removing the addictive effects of obsessive thought patterns. This is something that is frequently overlooked by those trying to help people with obsessive thought tendencies. Being obsessive and being addicted are very similar. Being addicted to something means that the body-mind system has become dependent on a particular form of stimulation. Take the stimulation away and there will be withdrawal symptoms, maybe powerful, even serious. Many drugs are known for their powerful addictive effects. White Dead Nettle helps to break the addictive aspects of thought patterns which can lock us in just as surely as addictive drugs.

OXALIS* *(Oxalis pes-caprae)*
This beautiful pure yellow flower is widespread in many parts of the world. It can be found in places as far apart as Bermuda and South Africa. Its essence is for things that "have you by the throat". When people feel to be in the clutches of something that is strangling them, holding them back, this is the essence to choose. Often the fear of feeling strangled will have caused constriction in the throat area and this constriction will have magnified the symptoms. Oxalis helps to unblock the energy in the Throat Chakra. As the throat area frees up, the nature of the threatening forces can be more readily discerned. With this information people can usually see the best way of extricating themselves from their difficulties. Oxalis can be of great help to people who have difficulties in either allowing new things to enter their lives or in relinquishing the old ones. Often the use of Milk Thistle will encourage the inhibiting fears to release their hold.

PINE CONES *(Pinus sylvestris) (F) (A) - Component of Self-Esteem*
The essence of Pine Cones is for those who feel trapped by the authoritarian power of others and are unable to escape.
The source of these feelings of inadequacy, and the need for the approval of others, can usually be traced back to childhood. There may be such a lack of self-confidence that the ability to express personal authority may well be nearly impossible. In adolescence, the inhibiting forces may have been so great that the normal changeover from parental authority to self-authority has not taken place. Perhaps there was a dominant parent who was over-protective, preventing the child from making its own decisions and thereby learning from its own mistakes. If the dominant authoritarian power came from a priesthood, then there may well be fears of evil, of the devil, or of losing one's soul, unless one does exactly as one is told. To those who have been heavily dominated, the world can seem to be such a frightening place, that they need to turn to others for help and reassurance.
The Pine Cones essence helps to free us from worrying about pleasing others. This automatically leads us to an understanding that "authorities" are simply people - people who indeed may well know

less about the truth of things than we do! The opinions of others are then seen in their true perspective. Pine Cones helps to open us to the realisation that, in breaking free from the authoritarian control of others, all we lose are our chains.

PINK PURSLANE* *(Montia siberica)*

This essence relates to our views of reality, how we see the world and how we relate to it.

Many of us grow up with views of the world that are heavily influenced by the attitudes of our parents, teachers and peers. These may or may not be fallacious. In any case they are views inherited by others, not gained from our own experience and insight. Such knowledge can be deeply flawed, yet human nature is such that our conscious mind will readily paper over the cracks so that we remain unaware of the flaws. This is why so many people grow up accepting in the religious and political views of their parents. Pink Purslane gently allows us to evaluate our belief structures from a point of insight and compassion. It is never easy to admit that the things that we have clung to for so long may just not be true. That is why self-compassion is needed and this beautiful small pink flower radiates that energy very powerfully. Seeing ourselves and our beliefs with true insight could be a pretty frightening experience. Pink Purslane lovingly helps us to steadily loosen our grip until we finally realise that all we were clinging to were illusions that we have now outgrown. It is a flower of freedom. It helps us to find new and wider horizons and richer and more fulfilling ways of living. It is gentle yet very persistent!

PROTECTION & CLEARING*

BLACK LOCUST *(Robinia pseudoacacia L.)*, SCARLET PIMPERNEL *(Anagallis arvensis)*, LICHEN *(Marchantia polymorpha L.)*, WHITE CHERRY *(Prunus taihaku)*

This composite essence clears negative energies and protect us from negative outside influences.

Black Locust is the key essence for protecting us from outside negative influences - including "psychic attack". At the same time this beautiful flower radiates healing energies to those who might otherwise take energies from us, whether consciously or otherwise.

Scarlet Pimpernel frees us from negative influences from other people, usually someone close to us. It helps us to find the inner strength to let go of unhealthy relationships, whilst preventing the other person from noticing the liberating changes that are taking place within us.

Lichen mirrors symbiosis - that of two different energies working happily together. It helps us to live happily in our environment. When we are at ease with our surroundings we naturally feel happier, more inspired and fulfilled.

White Cherry is for cleansing - washing away negative influences from the past. All of us, from time to time, find old reaction patterns from the past affecting our lives. Sometimes the root cause may not be at all obvious. White Cherry helps these old energy patterns, locked in the cells of the body, to reduce and finally dissipate, leaving us free to live our lives much more fully.

RAGWORT *(Senecio jacobaea) - Component of Obsession*

Ragwort helps us to tackle problems at their roots. It interrupts the endless looping thoughts that otherwise tend to feed on themselves.

Obsession is caused by a feedback system that has become unstable. Our thoughts try to find answers to our difficulties, but the effort always leads back to the beginning, where we start the same process all over again. It is as if we are playing a game of snakes and ladders where all the last six squares have a snake that takes us back to the beginning!

Ragwort has two properties that can help us. First it works to remove the emotional kick that we get from obsessive thoughts. Often it is the emotion that keeps the thoughts running. Second, it is a strong tough plant. That quality of strength can support us in the change period whilst we readjust to having a much quieter mind. It may seem surprising, but a quiet mind can feel quite alien and distressing when we have become accustomed to the constant mind chatter of obsessive thoughts. We need to learn how to manage without a constant emotional stimulus and Ragwort can be very useful in enabling that change to take place with the minimum of difficulty.

RED CLOVER *(Trifolium pratense) - Component of Yang*
This is for those who are emotionally blocked off through a deep-rooted fear of the emotional side of their nature.
Many people fear the serious damage that unbridled emotions can bring. This can lead to their suppressing their emotions in the belief that this will prevent a hidden aspect of their nature causing problems. The problem is that in so doing they greatly reduce their enjoyment of life.

Red Clover gently encourages the emotional side to emerge. It is important that this change is gradual so that the changes can be integrated without stress. The usual indications of emotional blockage are when someone appears hard, cold and calculating; and everything is directed to utilitarian ends. In these cases "art for art's sake", just "watching the world go by", or doing "useless" things may appear to be a total waste of time. Here the problem is usually due to a largely blocked-off right (intuitive) brain function. Red Clover encourages communication between the two sides of the personality. The left (logical) brain will then begin to allow and trust the activities of the right brain and finally rejoice that it has such an amazing partner to work with!

RED FRANGIPANI* *(Frangipani plumeria rubra)*
This beautiful fragrant flower has the power to reunite us with the source of our being. Believing in a God, Allah, Great Spirit, Buddha-Nature (call it what you will) is one thing. Actually experiencing such a contact is a totally different matter. The ego knows that in such experience it will inevitably begin to dissolve and disappear. This creates deep fears. It has been likened to the fear that a raindrop could feel when it falls towards a river where it knows it will merge and disappear into a greater unity.

In our heart of hearts we know that there is more to life than just physical existence. Frangipani helps to unlock this area of our being.

This will inevitably generate both joy and fear as the bonds that have limited us begin to let go. Red Frangipani lessens the fears of such revelations, by helping us to recognise that the ego has been blinding us to our true destiny. We will then begin to understand our true nature. This essence is about lightness of living and clarity of vision. It brings joy and ease, true self-confidence and new levels of perception.

Feeling isolated from our source inevitably causes us distress, even though we may fail to recognise the reasons for our difficulties. It is for this reason that many people look for satisfaction in ever-increasing possessions or power. Frangipani helps us by bringing a truer sense of perspective. It brings a lightness of touch - a very necessary balm in times of trouble.

It is the essence of true awakening.

RED POPPY *(Papaver argemone) - Component of Anger & Frustration*
The Red Poppy essence stabilises fire energy, the creative life-force that needs to be under our control at all times.

It is vital for our comfort and happiness that we harness our energies in ways that are beneficial rather than harmful. Fire energy out of control can be destructive to ourselves as well as others. It is, however, the driving force behind all that we do: too little fire and we become ineffective, too much and we become destructive. Red Poppy helps to stabilise our fire energy, preventing us from becoming excessively angry or turning our anger inwards. It assists us to grasp situations more accurately so that we can decide on the most appropriate form of action. Sometimes we may need to express our feelings openly, sometimes it may be prudent not to do so. Perhaps we are faced with a situation that appears to be intolerable, yet we may be in a position where making a hostile response could cause serious repercussions (perhaps, for instance, losing our job). Controlling our energies is a Red Poppy quality which prevents us from going into a self-destruct mode out of frustration. It will help us to acknowledge that in such cases we are powerless to change our circumstances. We can therefore channel our energies in a more positive manner, perhaps looking towards ways of changing our circumstances later on. Red Poppy is thus a very positive healing essence that can make our life much easier, and also much easier for those around us!

RHODODENDRON *(Rhododendron ponticum) - Component of Stuck in a Rut*

Rhododendron is for those who have not learned how to solve problems in their lives.

It may be that in childhood they became conditioned into the idea that, with sufficient application and energy, there is an answer to everything. The problem with this approach is that when things do not happen as we expect, we will try harder and harder to force a solution.

We need is a sense of proportion, the gift of being able to stand back and look carefully at the whole situation. With such a detached viewpoint we may well see that we are either attempting the impossible or using the wrong methods in trying to achieve our ends.

An example is that of the student who stays up all hours trying to cram for an examination. The harder he tries, the more his mind refuses to take in information. He may even precipitate a nervous breakdown.

The same characteristic can be seen in politicians who try to solve a problem by "throwing money at it". Understanding the nature of the problem itself is what is really needed, rather than using a simplistic made-to-measure approach.

Rhododendron helps us to see problems in a wider context and to ask questions about the situation. Maybe the problem is insoluble - considering the time and money available. Maybe we are trying to solve the wrong problem!

Problems in our life can be many and various. They may be spiritual, physical or interpersonal. Whatever our problems and difficulties the same basic skills are needed: to be able to detach ourselves from emotional entanglement with a problem and see things from a wider viewpoint. Rhododendron can greatly help us to develop this vital life skill.

ROSEBAY WILLOWHERB *(Chamaenerion angustifolium) - Component of Confusion*
Rosebay Willowherb is the essence needed when we seem to be blown about by every wind of change.
When we seem to be at the mercy of the world around us, impotent in the face of external circumstances, we can feel deeply depressed and confused. When this happens there is usually a complete lack of "earthing" energy. Like the down of the Willowherb in the autumn, we are blown hither and thither by the forces that surround us. We feel very unsure of ourselves and of the world around us. We find ourselves confused about where we are in life and what we should be doing. Nothing seems stable and reliable any more.
The essence of Willowherb helps us to root ourselves firmly in the world and our present situation. It gives us stability and strength. Only when we are stable and quiet can we truly evaluate the situation that we find ourselves in. Willowherb also helps us to energise our new-found stability so that we can then go out into the world with renewed confidence.
The essence of Mediterranean Sage may well be helpful if taken at the same time.

ROUND HEADED LEEK* *(Allium sphaerocephalum L.)*
This tiny member of the onion family grows in Cyprus. The essence made from it is very useful for those who have difficulties relating to childhood, without being able to pin down what the problems are.
Childhood is frequently a source of difficulties that emerge later in life. Many things get buried in our sub-conscious, bearing negative fruits later on. The art is to be able to understand them but with the insights of a mature adult, rather than regressing and reliving them through the eyes of a disempowered child. There are many satisfactory ways of going beyond known childhood difficulties, yet problems that do not surface in the conscious mind can be very difficult to deal with. Here the Round Headed Leek comes into its own. This essence helps to neutralise the forces (usually of fear) that are holding old patterns within the unconscious areas of the mind.

Once we can see these old patterns and identify them, then it is much easier to release them. The Round Headed Leek helps to bring those old repressed energies to the surface. It also enables us to see that whatever happened to that child did not happen to the adult - we have moved on and the childhood situation no longer exists. With that insight the old repressed energies evaporate as they no longer have anything to hold on to.

An essence of compassionate understanding, such as Wild Rose, may be very helpful if taken at the same time.

SACRED LOTUS* (Nelumbo nucifera)

This beautiful flower encourages the blossoming of personal growth. It helps to open the heart to the love of the Universe and the Divine.

Many people seek knowledge of the divine, the force that lies behind everything in the universe. To try to understand it they have called it by names such as God, Allah, Nirvana, The Great Spirit, etc. The trouble with all such names is that people then try to interpret the name in ways that they can understand.

The Sacred Lotus is well named. It helps to open our heart to the ultimate reality, by whatever name you might wish to call it. This is a powerful essence yet it will not do the bidding of the ego. It allows us to develop at a safe pace. If we try to open up to higher levels of consciousness too rapidly, we may well become distressed and confused. There is a saying in the East, "Softly softly catchee monkey". We need to remember this and not be too impatient in our spiritual development. All flowers take time to grow and our blossoming comes from living in the physical earth. Like the Lotus we first need to be rooted firmly in the Earth plane before we can safely start growing towards the light.

Like all flower essences, the intelligence within the essence knows what we need at any particular time. We cannot force progress. This essence encourages the flowering of our personal growth. It opens us up to the love of the infinite and at the same time helps us to re-radiate that love to the world around us.

SADNESS & LONELINESS*
COMPACT RUSH *(Juncus conglomeratus)*, DOG ROSE *(Rosa canina)*,
HONEYSUCKLE *(Lonicera periclymenum)*
Sadness and loneliness can have a devastating effect on our lives.
We can feel wholly dispirited and bereft. We need a new viewpoint, a
new and transforming way of seeing the world.

Compact Rush is for sadness, for those who feel that life is passing
them by. They dwell on what might have been and may feel that their
life is now pointless. Compact Rush is about wiping the slate clean,
about new beginnings and renewed energy. It helps us look on our
past with compassion, rather like seeing an old movie that we once
took part in. It is through detachment that we are freed from its
influence.

Dog Rose, as in the Grief composite, is included for its loving
support properties. This is something that we dearly need at such
times in our life. When we are sad and lonely, without realising it we
isolate ourselves from the world. Dog Rose helps us to become open
again to the love of the world around us.

Honeysuckle of the hedgerows perfumes the air around it in the
evening. This essence is included to help our fragrance to spread all
around us, drawing others to us. Sadness and loneliness tend to
isolate us from others. Honeysuckle helps reverse this, changing our
attitude to life so that others are drawn to us, helping us to feel a
valued part of humanity once more.

SCABIOUS *(Knautia arvensis) - Component of Shock & Trauma*
Scabious initiates the healing process after serious shock or
trauma. It helps us to accept what has happened to us and brings
comfort and ease to the healing process.

When we have been subjected to serious upset, particularly when
there has been injury to the mind or body, then the natural healing
processes can be severely disrupted. A shocked mind can easily inhibit
the healing that would otherwise naturally take place.

Scabious gently helps us to accept what has happened, whatever the
apparent consequences, so that our distress does not block the natural
healing.

In addition Scabious brings its own unique healing energies into play, opening our consciousness to love and compassion. Whatever has happened, there is no point in having regrets. We can only go on into the future as well as we can. Scabious also helps us to see that even serious problems may have very positive outcomes that we cannot possibly envisage at the time. It enables us to keep going even when the going is very rough.

SCARLET PIMPERNEL *(Anagallis arvensis)*
Component of Liberation and Protection & Clearing

Scarlet Pimpernel is a useful essence for someone emotionally entangled with another person.

There are two states the flower deals with - either being obsessed or being "possessed" by someone else. In either case they are unable to break free, even though they may realise that the relationship is unsatisfactory and probably very bad for them. There may well be strong psychic bonds originating from the dominant person. These can be difficult to break as this person usually has a lot to gain from the possessive relationship. Often there is a deep-rooted fear in the victim of breaking free from this connection in case it leaves them void and desolate. In addition, they know that they will have to face the anger of the other person. Domination by others saps our will-power and subverts our energies. The process frequently starts when someone seems to offer us something that we want or feel we need - for example, love, sex, money or spiritual growth. We fail to see that sometimes the person offering us these things is, in some way, a predator, and that we may well become a victim if we fall under their spell.

Scarlet Pimpernel works at a hidden level, enabling us to disconnect the ties that bind us and to gain sufficient power to break free. Early Purple Orchid may well be helpful if taken at the same time. This will help to open up the energy channels to the changes that are taking place.

SEA CAMPION* *(Silene maritima)*

This essence is for those who suffered separation early on in their lives. Whilst this is most frequently due to a separation from the mother, a separation from the protective male energy of the father can also cause trauma. All human babies, and many animal ones, need a close bond with their mothers during the early stages of life. This builds up a sense of security and of being cared for and loved. That in turn gives a strong firm base for the infant to grow up from, feeling secure in the world in which it finds itself. As well as the loving maternal background, babies also need the feeling of firm protective energy around them. Ideally this comes from the father, but can be provided by some equally supportive Yang energy.

If a loving stable background is weak or missing, then children feel insecure and fearful. This can lead to nightmares and bed-wetting in childhood. When they are older, they may have deep-rooted feelings of insecurity and be dogged by fears. Such fears can greatly disempower them, preventing them from expressing themselves properly in the world.

Sea Campion is a flower that relates to the Earth element. If we are properly "earthed", then we will be in harmony with nature. We will then have strong roots that enable us to withstand "the slings and arrows of outrageous fortune", as Shakespeare put it. The element Earth is to do with nurturing, with being at home in situations, with belonging to this Earth that is our present home. Sea Campion is therefore a flower that helps us return to our roots, to find contentment and peace in the world. It grows on bleak windswept cliffs that are battered by the winter storms, yet it still blossoms in the spring. Sea Campion is a "Return to Earth" flower, helping to bring ease to the insecure heart.

SELF-ESTEEM*
BUTTERBUR *(Petasites hybridus)*, MOSS *(Discranella heteromalla)* (P) (A), PINE CONES *(Pinus sylvestris)* (F) (A), WITCH HAZEL *(Hamamelis mollis)*

Many people suffer from low self-esteem and it does not always show up as subservience. Over-aggressive behaviour shows a lack of self-esteem just as surely.

Butterbur is for those who have had their self-esteem damaged from an early age. They may well feel inadequate because of adverse comments from parents and teachers early in their lives. They may have become convinced that in some way they are unworthy. Butterbur liberates and opens the way for the discovery of innate strengths and wisdom.

Moss is for those who fear the dark spaces within their being. They do not recognise their innate goodness, surrounded as it may be by a mass of negative conditioning. Moss helps us to see that it is only our fears that we are really frightened of, and that such fears disappear as we discover more and more of our true being.

Pine Cones is an essence for those who feel trapped by the authoritarian powers of others. They fail to recognise their own authority and seek the approval of others for all that they do. Pine Cones helps us to discover our own powers and authority and so leave subservience behind.

Witch Hazel is for those who are always trying to live up to the expectations of others. Because they feel that they must never fail to help others, they drive themselves relentlessly. Witch Hazel helps them to break this circle of dependence and take a more relaxed view, thereby stopping trying to help others who are perfectly capable of helping themselves!

SHEEP'S SORREL *(Rumex acetocella)* - *Component of Grief*

Sheep's Sorrel is for bitterness, the type of bitterness that arises when we feel that life is unfair. It is for the anguished cry of "Why should this have happened to me?"

Life has a nasty habit of upsetting our plans and expectations: we often have a feeling that it should be fair, forgetting that "fairness" is a human concept.

In this life everything changes ceaselessly. A period of calm will never last indefinitely, nor will times of difficulty. Accepting the endless ebb and flow of life can be difficult for us as we all look for stability. When something very traumatic happens, such as a bereavement or separation, we can so easily feel bitter about what has happened. Such bitterness can hang on, poisoning our life. Sheep's Sorrel helps us to accept what has happened and to understand that what now matters is the life ahead of us, even though it inevitably be different from what we had expected. It encourages us to let go of bitterness and to move forward into a new and changed future.

SHOCK AND TRAUMA*
STAR OF BETHLEHEM *(Ornithogalum arabica)*, IVY *(Hedera helix)*, SCABIOUS *(Knautia arvensis)*

When circumstances around us suddenly change, we can become very shocked. Whatever the cause, three things are needed to help us emerge from our traumas as rapidly and easily as possible. These are covered by three essences.

Star of Bethlehem is for immediate shock reaction. The emotional kick-back from sudden shock can have a devastating effect on our whole system, even causing us to faint. Star of Bethlehem works to cancel this immediate shock reaction, helping us to become more detached from what has actually happened.

Ivy is to help us remain grounded and at ease. To resist the negative effects of what has happened we need to be solidly rooted in the present moment, tenaciously holding on to life. For this Ivy is an excellent remedy.

Scabious is to help restore us with its gentle healing properties. It enables us to accept and perhaps learn from what has happened without emotional entanglement. Scabious brings ease and comfort to the shaken being.

SIBERIAN SPRUCE *(Picea omorica)* - *Component of Yang*
This is for those whose Yang "male" energy is low. It is the essence to choose for a lack of assertiveness. Many people prefer to take a low profile rather than come up-front and accept personal responsibility for their actions. Sensitive people, whose Yin "feminine" aspect is dominant, often have difficulties in dealing with the Yang side of their nature. It is the opposite of the Red Clover personality. They are equally unbalanced but in opposite directions. Here it is a fear of being exposed to the hard light of reality that is the problem. Often there is an exaggerated emotional response to life. What is needed is a firm unshakeable grounding energy, and Siberian Spruce points the way to this. Many people have the mistaken belief

that the Rambos of this world represent the true male aspect, whereas in fact they represent the negative aspects of the male. The positive male aspects of uprightness, openness and outgoingness are the qualities encouraged by this essence. Siberian Spruce helps to lift the Yang energies up to balance those of the Yin.

SINGLE SNOWDROP* (Galanthus nivalis) is also a component of Transition

Single Snowdrop is for those who are experiencing difficulties in breaking through to new levels of consciousness and awareness. It is the essence for those who seem to have encountered a barrier or block on their path towards personal freedom. It may well be that old habitual patterns of behaviour feel under threat and so they react negatively in an attempt to remove that threat. The net result is that efforts to change positively are continually being subverted. There can also be reactions against increasing insight. Seeing things more clearly can, at first, give the impression that the world is a bleak place (rather like the world which the snowdrop sees as it emerges in the late winter). Single Snowdrop helps to reveal the joyful potential of a true and wider vision. Old negative set ways can then be seen for what they really are - apparently comfortable strait jackets!

The transition of accepting one's spiritual nature, whilst remaining firmly rooted in the world, is not easy. Because Single Snowdrop mirrors the struggle of our spiritual nature to emerge and blossom, we chose this flower to be our logo.

SOAPWORT (Saponaria ocymoides) - Component of Confusion

Soapwort is the essence that is needed when we are bewildered and confused. There is a feeling of "What the hell am I doing here?" that is usually followed by the unspoken question of "How do I get out?" This state is often encountered during personal development as the older identities lose their grip and fall away. The loss of the old personal self-image can be a time of distress and trauma, when the new has not yet fully emerged. It is in this personal "void" that many deep positive changes can take place, so what is needed is encouragement. The feeling of "better the devil you know rather than the one you don't" can so often take over at this time. Soapwort prevents us from falling back into these old ways. It can be viewed as helping to wash away the past negative influences and providing love and encouragement for embracing the new.

SOLOMON'S SEAL* *(Polygonatum verticillatum)*

This is the essence for the "busy" person who has things that need doing but who somehow cannot get round to completing them. All too often we get bogged down with trivia, unable to settle to the more essential jobs in a clear and competent manner. We do not see that it is the act of being busy that is the real problem. By becoming quiet and apparently doing less, we actually become much more efficient, spending far less time and energy doing things in an inappropriate way. Indeed, we should question the need for doing some things at all! This busy-ness is often exploited by other people who see us as a soft touch, using us to do what they want, irrespective of our own needs. As we quieten, we increasingly discover what we need to be doing for our own fulfilment. Less and less will we automatically agree to the requests of others.

This essence can also be very helpful to those who practise meditation but who have problems with a constantly chattering mind, a very common complaint. Our minds should be our servants, not our masters. Solomon's Seal helps us to reassert control over our wayward minds. It is rather like training an unruly dog, so it may take an appreciable time. However, the end result is well worth the time taken.

SPEEDWELL* *(Veronica persica) – also in Unification*

Speedwell is about increasing our receptivity. It represents the "All-seeing Eye" of eastern philosophy, bringing insight in such a way that it seems entirely natural. It is concerned with maintaining our equanimity within meditation so that we do not get emotionally involved with the insights that may be revealed to us.

There are always difficulties when we try to expand our consciousness. It is all too easy for the ego, i.e. what we believe ourselves to be, to get in the way. This is an area where it is easy to get bogged down in religious fanaticism. Our minds can have a difficult job in trying to interpret information coming from a totally different level of consciousness: inevitably there will be errors in the translation. For example, a transcendental experience could be interpreted by a Buddhist as seeing the Buddha or by a Muslim as seeing Allah. Our conditionings or beliefs affect our interpretations. Speedwell gives us a clarity of vision whereby we become less inclined to apply stereotyped interpretations to the information that we receive from higher realms of consciousness. It helps us to open up to these higher levels of consciousness whilst keeping our feet firmly on the ground, without being swayed by personal opinions.

SPOTTED ORCHID* *(Dactylorhiza fuchsii)*

This small pyramidal orchid grows in damp places, flowering in similar habitats to Bog Asphodel. Indeed, in some locations they can be seen flowering together.

Sooner or later, all those who have embarked on a path of personal growth will meet a block. Frequently this block is the unspoken question "Where do I go from here?" At such points we can feel lost and bewildered, sometimes wondering whether we have done a wise thing in setting out on our quest at all. Often this is where we turn to a teacher or guru figure. The help gained from others can be problematical, however, depending on where we are and where they are, on our respective paths.

Personal growth and evolution are rather like finding our way through a large maze. There are dead ends, loops back along the path, and dangers as well. Not really for the faint-hearted! That is why we all need help and encouragement from time to time. We are, after all, human, with very real needs. Yet the rewards of following a personal quest are incalculable.

Spotted Orchid can provide support and guidance, sometimes pointing us to another part of our personal maze that we need to explore. It is not necessarily an easy essence to work with. It can make us afraid if it prompts us to "go out on a limb" and we have to accept responsibility for it. Yet it also supports us in our quest for our own personal "holy grail". Above all it empowers us, helping us to have the courage of our convictions and to converse more easily with our own soul essence.

Spotted Orchid can be seen as rather like an emissary of the Truth, mirroring our Soul Desire and Divine Will. It can guide us, encourage and support us, but we have to do all the hard work!

SPRING SQUILL* *(Scilla verna) - also a component of the Transition essence*
For those who are breaking through to new freedoms - the "Jonathan Livingstone Seagulls" of this world. These are the ones who are finding joy in realising that they really can be free, where previously they had been limited by old ideas and concepts. Sometimes this transition is difficult. There may be pressure from family, peer groups, friends, etc. who find the new ways very threatening and who may try nearly anything to prevent or reverse the change. Those breaking through into new freedoms often need support for their vulnerable self-confidence. It can seem quite lonely, flying in freedom, apparently alone. Spring Squill, relating as it does to the Crown Chakra, can assist in this. From the viewpoint of freedom, the world is then seen as it is: an amazing workshop for emerging souls. Without that insight, our fears and attitudes may well paint it as a dark and fearsome place, to endure or to escape from. Spring Squill helps us to see more widely and deeply into the true nature of reality. This remedy is most effective when other major blockages (particularly at the heart centre) have been eased. Only when the groundwork has been done can a person begin to fly in freedom.

STAR OF BETHLEHEM *(Ornithogalum arabica) - Component of Shock & Trauma*
Star of Bethlehem is used as the basic shock essence, taking the initial negative reaction out of the system. This is vital in severe cases.
When we are shocked the whole of the body's nerve system is severely upset. The initial shock reaction affects all the cells in the body and completely disrupts the body's energies. Indeed, people often die more from shock than they do from injury in severe accidents. Shock tends to make us detach and give up the will to live. Our Star of Bethlehem is made as a sun essence and it helps the mind to let go of the immediate traumatic experience. This is vital as it

takes the sting out of the experience and so greatly reduces the body's shock reaction. Wherever there is sudden shock, this is the essence of choice for use immediately after the experience.

This is the reason why Star of Bethlehem is included in the Shock & Trauma essence; it is the essential first aid part of the composite.

STUCK IN A RUT*

DOUBLE SNOWDROP *(Galanthus nivalis "flore-plena"),* MARSH THISTLE *(Cirsium palustre),* SUMACH *(Rhus typhina)* (L), RHODODENDRON *(Rhododendron ponticum)*

This is for those who have become bogged down in life. They have somehow become the victims of fixed routines and also perhaps become locked in the desire for security.

Double Snowdrop is for those who have become set in their ways and see no real need to change, or are frightened of what changes might bring into their life. Double Snowdrop shows us that change is essential if we are to live our lives to the full and it helps to initiate changes.

Marsh Thistle is for those who have become locked in the past and pay little attention to the present. It helps us to see we have imprisoned ourselves by doing this. Marsh Thistle leads us into a much more joyful way of life, living for the present moment.

Sumach is for those who refuse to accept their own true potential. "People like me can't do things like that" is a common response. All of us have enormous potential and Sumach encourages us to open up to those much greater realities.

Rhododendron is for those who try to make things happen the way they would like them to do. They try to make things fit in with their ideas, rather than feeling into the situation they are faced with. Childhood or adolescent conditioning is frequently the cause. Rhododendron helps us to develop a more relaxed approach to life, and stop trying to push square pegs into round holes.

SUMACH *(Rhus typhina) (L) (A) - Component of Stuck in a Rut*

Sumach is the essence for those who steadfastly refuse to accept their own potential.

Many gifted people hide their light under a bushel and try to pretend that it does not exist. There are many different reasons for this. It could be that much dedicated work or a considerable financial input is needed. Perhaps their partner is deeply opposed to it. Maybe there is a problem of self-image such as "People like me can't do things like that", or the defensive "Others do these things far better than I ever could". These are usually just excuses put up by the conscious mind. The reality is that they are frightened of owning up to their full powers and potential. In accepting their true role in life they would have to accept a new self-image - that of a powerful adult. They would then have to come out into the open, which could well make them feel very vulnerable. Sumach shows them that there is no hiding place and that it takes far less energy to accept what one is than waste energy in trying to oppose it. When they finally accept the truth the reaction is always the same - "Why did I put up so many barriers to change, when life is so much more rewarding this way?" Sumach helps them to reveal their true selves.

THRIFT* *(Armeria maritima)*

This essence is indicated for stabilisation of the psychic areas of insight. It is the essence for those whose psychic gifts are developing, but who need this development to be strongly "earthed". As a tree cannot grow to maturity without firm roots, so we must be strongly rooted in ordinary everyday life before it is safe to open up to other aspects of reality. Some people tend to go "over the top" in the psychic areas and become very emotionally involved in beliefs and concepts. Thrift stabilises them so that the psychic gifts can develop in balance with other aspects of the personality. These gifts will then be seen as neither more nor less "spiritual" than those in any other area. For many, this earthing is very necessary. Opening up to psychic areas without sufficient grounding can easily give rise to deep fears or other forms of vulnerability. Thrift helps to establish a strong, safe base for our inner development. This essence can be very helpful to those who work as healers or teachers and who find that they tend to take on the symptoms of their clients. In chakra terms, this essence relates to stabilising the energy flows between the Brow and Root centres.

TRAILING ST. JOHN'S WORT *(Hypericum humifusum) - Component of Grief*
Trailing St John's Wort is for healing, particularly where there is the emotional tension and desperation that are so often a part of grieving.

This tiny flower helps us to relax and distance ourselves from emotional trauma. When there has been a sudden shock in our life, such as that caused by bereavement, we need healing support (the word healing means to make whole again). When someone or something we love or value deeply has been taken from us we need gentle loving support, helping us to accept the changes that have been forced on us.

Trailing St John's Wort works gently but powerfully to ease the situation that is causing us so much grief. It helps us to rebalance and to see that there is a way forward, a way that is far brighter than we might believe while we are immersed in the depths of our despair.

TRANQUILLITY*
HEATH BEDSTRAW *(Galium saxatile)*, TREE MALLOW *(Lavatera arborea)*, FUJI CHERRY *(Prunus incisa)*
Many of us do not lead a tranquil life: we are always busy and do not find peace within that busy-ness. This essence encourages us to change our attitude to life and to find peace within the storms of everyday life. It does not force change on us.

Fuji Cherry is the key essence. This essence encourages both the mind and the body to relax so that we do not wind ourselves up unnecessarily. As we begin to calm down we gain new insights into our everyday life which enables us to do exactly the same work as before but without the emotional stress that comes from an over-tense mind.

Heath Bedstraw helps us to relax and trust our environment. It enables us to see that the world is not as threatening a place as it sometimes would seem. We become re-energised.

Tree Mallow is included for its healing and inspiring properties. As we become less tense there is always a danger that we lose our drive but Tree Mallow helps to regenerate it, this time from a more solid basis – a relaxed state of mind.

TRANSITION*
BISTORT *(Polygonum bistorta),* SINGLE SNOWDROP *(Galanthus nivalis),* SPRING SQUILL *(Scilla verna)*

This composite is designed to help those who are experiencing difficulty as a result of major changes in their lives. Whether those changes seem to be good or bad, such times can be extremely stressful.

Bistort is the key essence in this composite - helping us by giving loving comfort and support during the process of change. It is as if it gives us an "inner scaffolding" that prevents us going into total collapse or breakdown. It encourages us to go forward into a new and more rewarding future.

Single Snowdrop is included to give us the courage to go forward into a completely new situation. At such times we may feel very threatened by what faces us. Breakthrough into new levels of awareness may give us quite a shock. Single Snowdrop helps us to accept our new situation with calm clarity.

Spring Squill encourages us to fly in freedom. While Bistort and Single Snowdrop help in the breaking through process, Spring Squill brings joy and exultation in the new freedoms that are opening up to us. It enables us to find our own true way, unencumbered by the attitudes and opinions of those around us.

TREE MALLOW *(Lavatera arborea) - Component of Tranquillity*

Tree Mallow is included because of its healing and inspiring properties. As we begin to relax more and more deeply, as we become more peaceful and tranquil, there is a risk that we may lose our power and drive: it may well have been largely our tensions that were driving us on. Tree Mallow facilitates healing and empowerment. Thus energised, we can go forward into life at the same time as we are becoming increasingly relaxed and tranquil. Tranquillity should not mean disempowerment, as is so often the case with tranquillising drugs. Rather it should mean that we become more powerful, as we have now reduced those tension patterns which had held us back. We only become tranquil and free when we can work from the present moment, from what exists in the "now". It is our fears that arise from past actions and future possibilities that prevent that vital relaxation occurring in our lives. Tree Mallow helps us to centre our attention more easily in the present moment. In reality, that is the only time that we ever have. We need to make the most of it.

TUFTED VETCH* *(Vicia cracca)*

The key remedy for many sexual difficulties. People frequently have a fairly mixed-up sexual self-image. This is hardly surprising considering the number of manipulative power games that are played out with sex as a basis. A wholesome human drive has variously been portrayed as dirty, obscene, something to lust for, manipulate others through, etc. With all the heavy conditioning from childhood onwards, many people have difficulties in this area. Sex, like money and power, has traditionally been used to manipulate people, and we grow up in an environment where such manipulation is widespread. Tufted Vetch helps us to rebalance our own sexual self-image in both male and female aspects. When this essence is indicated, it is worth looking to see whether either the Yin or Yang composite is needed, to bring the "male" and "female" characteristics into closer balance. As our own male and female sides become more balanced, we will find that much of the sting is taken out of our relationships with other people at a sexual level. Only when we are really at ease with our own sexuality will we find ease in relating sexually to other people. Only then can we truly honour our own sexuality and then, by reflection, honour the sexuality of others.

UNIFICATION*

FORSYTHIA *(Oleacea intermedia)*, NORWAY MAPLE *(Acer platanoides)*, ENGLISH OAK *(Quercus robur)*, SPEEDWELL *(Veronica persica)*

This helps to unify the mind-body spirit, helping us to break free of previous restricting beliefs and patterns.

Forsythia is about disentangling ourselves from an over-logical view of the world where the spiritual dimension is viewed with suspicion by the logical hemisphere of the brain. It also gives encouragement to those who have already discovered the path of self-realisation, bringing comfort and support during all the twists and turns of spiritual growth.

Norway Maple helps to free us rigid concepts so that the intuitive mind can explore the spiritual dimensions without the restricting influence of the logical mind.

Oak stimulates a quiet inner strength and a feeling of peace. Both of these qualities are necessary for the "Spiritual Warrior", the person who has embarked on the difficult journey to discover their true being. This essence embodies the quiet steadfastness needed for such a journey.

Speedwell mirrors the eastern concept of the "All-seeing eye" of the Brow Chakra. It enables us to open up our psychic senses in a gentle and matter-of-fact way showing us that insight is simply another, yet vital, aspect of ordinary everyday life. Speedwell is concerned with opening up our intuition without our getting emotionally entangled in what may be revealed to us.

VALERIAN *(Valeriana officinalis) - Component of Childhood*

Valerian is the essence for the "lost child" - someone who appears to be in need of help and support. Instinctively one feels one's heart go out to people like this - they seem so alone and helpless. In reality, direct help is probably not needed at all. Usually the original cause of the problem is a childhood deprived of true love. Although they may put a brave face on things, deep down they feel bereft and unable to love other people. They also know that something within them needs the love, support and encouragement that was not available to them when they were young. Valerian encourages the development of self-love and self-esteem, and gradually reduces the need for external support. This in turn reduces the demands made on others.

WELSH POPPY* *(Meconopsis cambrica)*

This is for those who have lost their fire and inspiration and have become day-dreamers. It is for those who have previously been energised and active, but whose driving energies have been dissipated. They have become side-tracked. Previous goals have lost their meaning. Sometimes this day-dreaming state is like following a path into a sunny field full of beautiful flowers. We get so carried away with lying in the sun and looking at the flowers that we forget there is a path that goes on beyond that field. People in this state frequently feel that their problems are due to the negative influence of others. In fact, the problem often relates to changing perceptions; old goals, now seen in a new light, lose their allure. Welsh Poppy helps to bring energy and inspiration back into our lives, to liberate blocked creative energies and it points us towards our true path.

WHITE DEAD NETTLE *(Lamium album) - Component of Obsession*

White Dead Nettle is about addictions to objects, events or people. Addictions and obsessions are closely interrelated.

We can become addicted to a person, perhaps a close friend or spiritual teacher. Under these circumstances we are giving away our control and power to them just as surely as we can to a drug.

We can become addicted to situations in life, whether it be the "high" of high-speed driving or as mundane as some comforting repetitive situation such as watching a favourite "soap" on television. The degree of personal danger and excitement is different, but the same factors are active in the background.

White Dead Nettle helps us to detach ourselves from emotional addiction. It does not mean we have to give up our favourite television watching, merely that we do not get so emotionally entangled.

WHITE CHERRY *(Prunus taihaku) – Component of Protection & Clearing*

This essence reaches deep into our being. It allows us to free ourselves from old patterns and negative influences from the past. From time to time all of us find ourselves in the grip of some emotion that has its roots in the long-distant past. Treating the emotion does not however solve the problem: unless the cause is removed, the emotional reaction will recur.

This particular White Cherry assists us by dissolving the old cellular memories that are behind our difficulties. These deeply rooted patterns from the past are imprinted in all our cells, hence the instantaneous shock that can accompany some of these old energies when they are triggered. In a strange way it is as if we are possessed by them.

White Cherry acts by gradually loosening the attachment to these old patterns until they finally dissipate - having been healed we are no longer bound to them.

This essence therefore has powerful cleansing and healing properties for old unresolved memory patterns.

WHITE LOTUS* (Nymphea alba)

This essence is about peace and tranquillity at all levels of consciousness. Whereas the Tranquillity composite is aimed at a lack of ease in the body-mind, White Lotus is about being at peace at every level of our being. It mirrors the tranquillity that can be experienced in deep meditation when all barriers have dissolved. Tensions, fears, beliefs and opinions are all released so that we can just be.

As an aid to meditation it can be very helpful in quieting the chattering mind. It can also act as an essence of purification by dissolving away things of our past that we no longer need. Its action may be mild or powerful, depending on circumstances. As usual, it depends on our personal motivation. Like all the other flower essences, it can only help us as far as we are prepared to go. We must also bear in mind that there is a safe maximum speed to progress.

White Lotus mirrors our resting at peace, sitting in quiet wonderment at the true beauty of everything in this astonishing universe. In this peace, attitudes and opinions ease away - finally leaving only pure consciousness, pure awareness. This flower represents the highest flowering of the human spirit when all that is unnecessary has fallen away.

WILD MALLOW (Malva sylvestris) - Component of Liberation

Within each of us there can be hidden possessive energies that try to control our life. These energies may originally relate to our parents who tried to dominate our lives, or to others who would try to control, and so "possess" us.

Wild Mallow brings these hidden possessive energies to the surface where we can see them. They can then be identified for what they really are, and in that revelation they lose their power over us. It is as if this essence tightens us up inside so that what is affecting us can be expelled. Rather like wringing out a cloth, the negative possessing energies are wrung out by Wild Mallow. For many people this may be the most important part of the combination essence Liberation. Seeing the reality of what is affecting us automatically empowers us. It is always the things hidden in the shadows, where we cannot see them, that cause the most problems.

WITCH HAZEL *(Hamamelis mollis) - Component of Self-Esteem*
Witch Hazel is for those who are always trying to live up to the expectations of others - the willing horses who are constantly trying to please their parents, teachers, partners, children, or whoever. You may find them on committees: the eager-beavers who are always busy and always helpful. They feel that to let anyone down is to fail, so they drive themselves relentlessly. This state often relates to childhood, when they felt that to keep their parents' approval they had to live up to their parents' expectations of them. This in turn gave rise to a conditioned response of always trying to gain the approval of others. They now need a wider view of the world, where they take their "mission" in life rather less seriously, ceasing to give themselves such a hard time. Witch Hazel helps the mind to drop its dependence on this continual stimulation and thus breaks the vicious circle. With progressive quietening and ease, a completely new evaluation of their lives then becomes possible.

WOOD ANEMONE* *(Anemone nemorosa)*
For problems where the roots are very old, often before birth. Some of these may well be karmic. "Acting completely out of character" can be an indication of this state. Where there are deep-rooted psychic problems, this is often the best remedy to start with. Sometimes people blame others for "psychic attack" without realising that they themselves may unwittingly have taken part in the process. There can be deep feelings of guilt and fear in such people, even though they have no idea why they are feeling fearful or guilty. Wood Anemone helps to clear these old blocked areas, illuminate them and so resolve the old tension patterns. Because of their very old origins,

karmic problems have gained the reputation of being difficult to eradicate. In fact, if we deal with any problem as it arises in this lifetime, any past difficulties will be resolved at the same time. It is in the present, not in the past, that we can rebalance our lives. As the constrictions become less pronounced, it becomes easier for us to perceive them. In seeing them and seeing how they affect our lives negatively, it becomes much easier to leave their influence behind. Monk's Hood can often be helpful when used at the same time.

Note on Yin and Yang Essences

The purpose of these two composites is to integrate the Yin and Yang qualities fully so that they can grow and develop together. This forms what has been called the alchemical marriage, where neither energy is predominant. This inner harmony will be reflected in the outside world, transforming our relationships with other people. We will then no longer be seduced into playing power games at sexual and personality levels. The strength and balance of the Yin-Yang partnership brings both empowerment and ease into our lives.

YANG*

SIBERIAN SPRUCE *(Picea omorica)*, YEW *(Taxus baccata)* (A) (L&F), NASTURTIUM *(Tropaeolum majus)*, RED CLOVER *(Trifolium pratense)*

To achieve balance, the Yang qualities in a person need to fulfil several different criteria. The fundamental property of Yang is concerned with personal power. It is about being able to make one's mark in the world. It is strong, steadfast and protective. These qualities are represented by Siberian Spruce.

The Yang energy can, however, become too rigid; it needs to be flexible yet strong. Without the ability to yield when necessary, Yang can make us domineering and dogmatic. This weakens us and makes us vulnerable to opposition. To give resilience and flexibility the essence of Yew is included.

When we need to make adjustments in our view of the world there can be problems if the Yang element is dominant. "Male pride" is a typical reaction against accepting changes, even when those changes are wise and necessary. Nasturtium gives help and support during such times - Yang energy is much more vulnerable than its outgoing quality might suggest at first sight.

Because of this it needs to build bridges with the Yin energies within the being. This is vital for both men and women. It is essential that Yang becomes open to suggestions from the intuitive Yin, which normally offers a much broader picture of what is going on. Without such communication, there will be unease within the being and this will be reflected into the outside world as unease in relationships with other people. For this aspect of the Yin-Yang partnership, Red Clover is included.

The Yang composite is therefore intended to assist the growth and balance of Yang energies so that they serve, rather than dominate, the being.

YEW *(Taxus baccata) (A) (L&F)* - Component of Yang

This essence is for resilience and for escaping from rigid patterns of thought and behaviour. Tensions make many people brittle and, although they may appear to be strong, they may suddenly crack under pressure. They are like cast iron which, although very strong, can fracture easily under a sudden shock. They may have developed strong principles about which they are very protective. This can result in their reacting fiercely against what they see as opposing forces. Yew helps people to see that there is no sin in being both resilient and flexible, or indeed bowing before the storm. It also brings the discernment needed to assess accurately just what forces are involved in any particular situation. After all, only a fool will stand in the path of an express train!

Yew helps people to become less proud of their own ideas and concepts, more open to new approaches and ideas, and break up the rigidity of outmoded patterns of thought and behaviour. It is a very useful essence for people who have become trapped by their own beliefs and opinions.

YIN*
LARCH (Alc.) *(Larix decidua),* MARIGOLD *(Calendula officinalis),*
DELPHINIUM *(Delphinium consolida),* HONESTY *(Lunaria annua)*
This essence comprises four flowers that mirror their counterparts in the Yang essence.

The alcoholic extract of Larch is concerned with female power. It is about intuition, feeling for what is going on underneath the surface. It is concerned with knowing how things are. It is also about love and compassion and nurturing. In its purest form it represents the Earth Mother. But this energy needs to be balanced or intuition can be replaced with make-believe.

Where there are difficulties or fears in opening up the Yin, Marigold can be of great assistance in unblocking the power of the Yin energies and then supporting them. In unblocking the channels, it paves the way for Larch to build on secure foundations. Marigold is therefore the opening-up and underpinning essence of the Yin composite.

Without guidance, the Yin insight can be narrow and shortsighted. In this it is like the male Yang with its tendency to tunnel vision. Such selective insight can prove to be disastrous. We need to be able to see the whole picture. Delphinium is concerned with higher levels of insight and enables us to see things from a much wider perspective than might otherwise be the case.

The last essence is Honesty and this helps the Yin to form links with the Yang. In this it mirrors the Red Clover in the Yang essence. The Yin can feel very threatened by the self-assurance of the Yang way of looking at things. Intuition, whether in men or in women, is often subjugated because of the feeling that the self-assured Yang energy must somehow be right. This can happen repeatedly even though our inner beings know that the intuition is right. It is therefore vital that the Yin learns to understand the Yang but is not overwhelmed by its outgoing energy.

YORKSHIRE FOG *(Holcus lanathus) - Component of Grief*
Yorkshire Fog enables us to open up to the pain of grief and to shed tears that help to wash away our anger, frustration and sadness.
Accepting our hurt and anguish is a very necessary part of the

healing process after bereavement or similar traumatic experiences. People bottle up their emotions because expressing their grief openly is not socially acceptable. But suppressing grief, trying to pretend that we are not seriously hurt, does not cure the problem. Burying our deep hurt merely means that it festers, sometimes for many years.

Yorkshire Fog helps us to open up to our grief, to express it openly, to weep cleansing tears. Grief is a natural reaction to what has happened to us. There is nothing weak or effeminate about expressing our grief openly, so long as we do not wallow in it.

Yorkshire Fog also helps us to move on from grieving to a new and changed future without feeling the need to drag the past along with us.

diagnostic groupings

Problems originating before conception	Wood Anemone
Problems stemming from the distant past	Monk's Hood White Cherry
Trapped by childhood patterns or difficulties	Bracken (Aqueous) Sea Campion Round Headed Leek Childhood
Lack of love in childhood	Milk Thistle Sea Campion
Locked in the past	Stuck in a Rut
Blocked or stunted in personal growth	Stuck in a Rut Self-Esteem Lilac
Underactive intuitive side (right brain)	Yin Thrift
Underactive logical side (left brain)	Yang Siberian Spruce
Confusion and bewilderment	Confusion Foxglove Spotted Orchid
Fears of the subconscious mind	Moss Cymbidium Orchid
Dogmatic or rigid opinions	Stuck in a Rut Yang Pink Purslane

Overactive mind	Obsession Solomon's Seal Tranquillity Fuji Cherry
Yearning	Lily of the Valley
Blocking of true personal power	Self-Esteem Butterbur
Lack of love or warmth in life	Buttercup Milk Thistle Mediterranean Sage
Need for comfort and support	Mediterranean Sage
Lack of openness	Yin
Sexual self-image difficulties	Tufted Vetch Dwarf Purple Vetch Yin Yang
Compulsive helping of others	Bog Asphodel Self-Esteem
Memory difficulties	Hairy Sedge
Unstable energy patterns	Anger & Frustration Firethorn
Major change point in life	Transition Early Purple Orchid Leopardsbane Bladder Senna Conifer Mazegill

Difficulty in moving forward in life	Yin Welsh Poppy Stuck in a Rut Fears
External opposition to change in life	Liberation Oxalis Scarlet Pimpernel
Loneliness, sadness, feeling deserted	Sadness & Loneliness
Depression about life	Depression Leopardsbane
Totally defeated in life	Depression Flowering Currant
Grief and anguish *Worries, fears, nightmares*	Grief Fears Cymbidium Orchid Cyprus Rock Rose
Sudden shock or trauma	Shock & Trauma Star of Bethlehem
Blocked energy flows in the body	Early Purple Orchid
Opening up to new levels of consciousness	Single Snowdrop Transition Spring Squill
Need for support through change	Bistort
Subconscious mind difficulties	Cymbidium Orchid Fears Spotted Orchid

Need for guidance and inspiration	Almond
	Spotted Orchid
Freedom from past restrictions	Spring Squill
	Liberation
	Meadow Rue
Protection from psychic disturbance	Black Locust
Ease and celebration on the path of personal growth	Arizona Fir
Unconditional love	Magnolia
Bringing forward energies from the past	Himalayan Blue Poppy
Rediscovering our true spiritual roots	Blue Pimpernel
Reuniting us with the source of our being	Red Frangipani
	White Lotus
	Sacred Lotus
Accessing true wisdom	Speedwell
Peace at all levels of our being	White Lotus

glossary
A-Z list of essences

Almond* *(Prunus dulcis)*

Anger and Frustration* *(Red Poppy, Firethorn, Holly Leaf)*

Arizona Fir* (A) *(Abies lasiocarpa var. compacta)*

Betony *(Stachys officinalis)* - Component of Fears

Bistort* (A) *(Polygonum bistorta)* - Component of Transition

Black Locust* *(Robinia pseudoacacia L.)* - Component of Protection & Clearing

Blackthorn *(Prunus spinosa)* - Component of Depression & Despair

Bladder Senna* *(Colutea orientalis)*

Bluebell *(Hyacinthoides non-scripta)* - Component of Depression & Despair

Blue Pimpernel* *(Anagallis arvensis var. caerulea)*

Bog Asphodel* *(Narthecium ossifragum)*

Bracken (Alc.) (A) (L) *(Pteridium aquilinum)* - Component of Childhood

Bracken (Aq.)* (L) *(Pteridium aquilinum)*

Butterbur *(Petasites hybridus)* - Component of Self-Esteem

Buttercup* *(Ranunculus acris)*

Charlock *(Sinapis arvensis)* - Component of Childhood

Childhood* *(Bracken Alc, Charlock, Valerian)*

Compact Rush *(Juncus conglomeratus)* - Component of Sadness & Loneliness

Confusion* *(Foxglove, Oak, Rosebay Willowherb, Soapwort)*

Conifer Mazegill* *(Gloeophyllum sepiarium)*

Cymbidium Orchid* (M) *(Cymbidium hybridus)*

Cyprus Rock Rose* *(Fumana arabica)*

Delphininum *(Delphinium consolida)* - Component of Yin

Depression & Despair* *(Blackthorn, Bluebell, Flowering Currant, Hawkweed)*

Dog Rose *(Rosa canina)* - Component of Grief and Sadness & Loneliness

Double Snowdrop *(Galanthus nivalis "flore-plena")* - Component of Stuck in a Rut

Dwarf Purple Vetch* *(Vicia villosa ssp. eriocarpa)*

Early Purple Orchid* *(Orchis mascula)*

Fears* *(Betony, Mahonia, Greater Celandine)*

Firethorn (F) (A) *(Pyracantha atalantioides)* - Component of Anger &
Frustration
Flowering Currant *(Ribes sanguineum)* - Component of Depression &
Despair
Forsythia *(Oleacea intermedia)* - Component of Unification
Foxglove *(Digitalis purpurea)* - Component of Confusion
Fuji Cherry *(Prunus incisa)* - Component of Tranquillity
Greater Celandine *(Chelidonium majus)* - Component of Fears
Grief* (Sheep's Sorrel, Dog Rose, Yorkshire Fog,
Trailing St John's Wort)
Hairy Sedge* *(Carex hirta)*
Hawkweed *(Hieracium vulgatum)* - Component of Depression &
Despair
Heath Bedstraw *(Galium saxatile)* - Component of Tranquillity
Himalayan Blue Poppy* *(Meconopsis betonicifolia)*
Holly Leaf (L) (A) *(Ilex aquifolium)* - Component of Anger &
Frustration
Honesty *(Lunaria annua)* - Component of Yin
Honeysuckle *(Lonicera periclymenum)* - Component of Sadness &
Loneliness
Indian Balsam *(Impatiens glandulifera)* - Component of Obsession
Ivy (L) (A) *(Hedera helix)* - Component of Shock & Trauma
Larch (A) *(Larix decidua)* - Component of Yin
Leopardsbane* *(Doronicum pardalianches)*
Lesser Stitchwort *(Stellaria graminea)* - Component of Liberation
Liberation* (Lesser Stitchwort, Scarlet Pimpernel, Wild Mallow)
Lichen *(Marchantia polymorpha L.)* - Component of Protection &
Clearing
Lilac* *(Syringa vulgaris "Massena")*
Lily of the Valley* *(Convallaria majalis)*
Magnolia* *(Magnolia x loebneri "Leonard Messel")*
Mahonia *(Mahonia aquifolium)* - Component of Fears
Marigold *(Calendula officinalis)* - Component of Yin
Marsh Thistle *(Cirsium palustre)* - Component of Stuck in a Rut
Meadow Rue* *(Phalictrum dipterocarpum)*
Mediterranean Sage* *(Salvia fruticosa)*

Milk Thistle* *(Sonchus oleraceus)*
Monk's Hood* *(Aconitum napellus)*
Moss (P) (A) *(Discranella heteromalla)* - Component of Self-Esteem
Nasturtium *(Tropaeolum majus)* - Component of Yang
Norway Maple *(Acer platanoides)* - Component of Unification
Oak (A) *(Quercus robur)* - Component of Confusion
Obsession* (Indian Balsam, Ragwort, White Dead Nettle)
Oxalis* *(Oxalis pes-caprae)*
Pine Cones (F) (A) *(Pinus sylvestris)* - Component of Self-Esteem
Pink Purslane* *(Montia siberica)*
Protection & Clearing* (Black Locust, Lichen, Scarlet Pimpernel, White Cherry)
Ragwort *(Senecio jacobaea)* - Component of Obsession
Red Clover *(Trifolium pratense)* - Component of Yang
Red Frangipani* *(Frangipani plumeria rubra)*
Red Poppy *(Papaver argemone)* - Component of Anger & Frustration
Rhododendron *(Rhododendron ponticum)* - Component of Stuck in a Rut
Rosebay Willowherb *(Chamaenerion angustifolium)* - Component of Confusion
Round Headed Leek* *(Allium sphaerocephalum L.)*
Sacred Lotus* *(Nelumbo nucifera)*
Sadness & Loneliness* (Compact Rush, Dog Rose, Honeysuckle)
Scabious *(Knautia arvensis)* - Component of Shock & Trauma
Scarlet Pimpernel *(Anagallis arvensis)* - Component of Liberation and Protection & Clearing
Sea Campion* *(Silene maritima)*
Self-Esteem* (Butterbur, Moss, Pine Cones, Witch Hazel)
Sheep's Sorrel *(Rumex acetocella)* - Component of Grief
Shock & Trauma* (Star of Bethlehem, Ivy, Scabious)
Siberian Spruce (F) (A) *(Picea omorica)* - Component of Yang
Single Snowdrop* *(Galanthus nivalis)* - Component of Transition
Soapwort *(Saponaria ocymoides)* - Component of Confusion
Solomon's Seal* *(Polygonatum verticillatum)*
Speedwell* *(Veronica persica)*
Spotted Orchid* *(Dactylorhiza fuchsii)*

Spring Squill* *(Scilla verna)* - Component of Transition
Star of Bethlehem *(Ornithogalum arabica)* - Component of Shock & Trauma
Stuck in a Rut* (Double Snowdrop, Marsh Thistle, Sumach, Rhododendron)
Sumach (L) (A) *(Rhus typhina)* - Component of Stuck in a Rut
Thrift* *(Armeria maritima)*
Trailing St John's Wort *(Hypericum humifusum)* - Component of *Grief*
Tranquillity* (Heath Bedstraw, Tree Mallow, Fuji Cherry)
Transition* (Single Snowdrop, Spring Squill, Bistort)
Tree Mallow *(Lavatera arborea)* - Component of Tranquillity
Tufted Vetch* *(Vicia cracca)*
Unification* (Forsythia, Norway Maple, Oak, Speedwell)
Valerian *(Valeriana officinalis)* - Component of Childhood
Welsh Poppy* *(Meconopsis cambrica)*
White Cherry *(Prunus taihaku)* - Component of Protection & Clearing
White Dead Nettle *(Lamium album)* - Component of Obsession
White Lotus* *(Nymphea alba)*
Wild Mallow *(Malva sylvestris)* - Component of Liberation
Witch Hazel *(Hamamelis mollis)* - Component of Self-Esteem
Wood Anemone* *(Anemone nemorosa)*
Yang* (Siberian Spruce, Yew, Nasturtium, Red Clover)
Yew (A) (F) *(Taxus baccata)* - Component of Yang
Yin* (Larch, Delphinium, Honesty, Marigold)
Yorkshire Fog *(Holcus lanathus)* - Component of Grief